RESIDENTIAL PROPERTY INVESTING
EXPLAINED SIMPLY

RESIDENTIAL PROPERTY INVESTING

EXPLAINED SIMPLY

STEVE PALISE

MAJOR
STREET

First published in 2022 by Major Street Publishing Pty Ltd
info@majorstreet.com.au | +61 421 707 983 | majorstreet.com.au

 A catalogue record for this book is available
from the National Library of Australia

Printed book ISBN: 978-1-922611-44-4
Ebook ISBN: 978-1-922611-45-1

Cover design by Tess McCabe
Internal design by Production Works
Part II illustrations by Simone Geary

10 9 8 7 6 5 4 3 2 1

CONTENTS

WHY RESIDENTIAL PROPERTY?

'A big part of financial freedom is having your heart and mind free from worry about the what-ifs of life.'
— Suze Orman

You may have read about me in my other book, *Commercial Property Investing Explained Simply*, but what I didn't tell you there is that while I have achieved fantastic financial success in the commercial property asset class, it all started in the residential market. I bought eight residential properties myself, and I secured around 1,000 properties for clients before making my first move into commercial, so you could say that houses were my first love.

I grew up in a gentrifying suburb of western Sydney. My father was a television repair technician, my mother was a stay-at-home mum and I have two older brothers (and even at 6 foot 3 inches tall, I'm by far the smallest of the bunch). At high school, I finished in the top one per cent of the state, and at the time I thought academic excellence would equate to wealth – and that wealth would bring happiness. I had a natural affinity for mathematics and theoretical concepts, which led me to study engineering at university, and I finished first in the course.

Specifically, I studied mechatronics, as my dream was to design robotic limbs for humans. But once I graduated, I realised sitting at a computer all day writing code was not for me.

I moved into mining and became a structural and mechanical design engineer, designing large industrial machines and mine sites. I began to earn good money and became one of the youngest engineers in Australia chartered in both mechanical and structural engineering.

What I enjoyed the most was spending one or two months on design work and then, three months later, this huge thing you have created is real and tangible. I loved design because, as in engineering, it offers little room for subjectivity. It all comes down to the numbers!

As an intern engineer in 2012, I was on $50,000 per year and starting to realise it was going to take me a long time to save decent money. So, while I was very nervous, I looked around the area I grew up in and took the plunge, buying my very first residential property – a house in Blacktown (in western Sydney, New South Wales). It cost $230,000, renting for $280 per week. I purchased the property on a 90 per cent loan with lenders mortgage insurance (LMI), so it cost me about $33,000 up front. The rent covered the mortgage, so it was 'set and forget', even though I had no idea whether the property would make a good long-term investment.

In the first year, I got that affirmation: the property value grew to circa $300,000 and I had made $70,000 from signing a piece of paper! This was my lightbulb moment, and from that moment on I was hooked. I read every book and listened to every podcast I could get my hands on, buoyed by the idea that there was no way I could save this profit on my salary – it would have taken at least five years.

Like many, though, I got caught up in the rat race. I was working long hours, earning a good salary and creating wealth, but I saw unqualified employees being promoted and earning high incomes while some of the most qualified employees were working hard but going unrewarded. My belief that academic excellence and hard work would be enough was shattered.

I decided that I didn't want my life as a professional to limit me, nor did I want to leave my financial future in the hands of a faceless corporate machine. So, I chose residential property as my path to financial independence. I saved incredibly hard and refinanced my first Blacktown property. However, I made some mistakes.

I bought my first property through my bank's local branch, so naturally I headed back there for my second purchase. I followed what my local bank manager recommended instead of speaking to a mortgage broker, as I should have. So, when I went to refinance my Blacktown property, with a lot of equity, the bank manager got me a 95 per cent loan and made me pay LMI again!

They could have given me an 80 to 90 per cent loan by refinancing more from my Blacktown property, but instead I basically paid LMI twice for no reason. They also cross-collaterised the properties so they were linked and the performance of one would affect how I could extract equity from the other.

After I found this out, I went to a different bank and spoke with their bank manager, who gave completely different advice. My lesson was to always use a broker and get more than one opinion.

As the Blacktown property kept growing in value, I began accumulating low-priced, positively geared properties. Every year I purchased more, and my portfolio grew exponentially. My best memory was when I sold a property and had half a million dollars in my bank account. As a 25-year-old engineer who was on about $100,000 a year at the time, this was such a feel-good moment. I had approximately 15 years' worth of savings in my account from investing well.

It was a big realisation that working nine to five for 40 years was not the best option moving forward. Off the back of my passive income from property, I bit the bullet, left my engineering career and went full-time into property. I became a buyer's agent, and within a few years I'd helped clients purchase more than 500 properties in the residential space.

When considering whether residential property investing is right for you, it's important to identify your happiness goals.

I'm not talking about a portfolio size or passive-income amount; most people overestimate what they need to be happy, and this leads them to take on unnecessary risk. Sacrificing time today to reach a specific number tomorrow is only worthwhile if that number delivers you tangible benefits. It's not about having hundreds of properties in your portfolio – it's purely about choice and freedom.

Assess your short-term, medium-term and long-term goals. What will make you happy? I've spoken to thousands of people from different walks of life, and everyone's compass for happiness is different; some are over the moon when they can afford a new fishing reel, others when they can purchase a $250,000 sports car. My own happiness comes from travelling, socialising, climbing mountains, feeling appreciated and working on passion projects. Property investing has enabled me to pursue these goals – I travelled, for example, to 35 countries by 35 years of age without sacrificing my professional career or my relationships. What will residential property investing help you achieve?

Benefits of residential property

Early on, I learnt some valuable lessons. As far as I could see, there was no other asset class that allowed you to maximise leveraging at 80 and 90 per cent. I learnt about the power of leveraging from all the real estate books, but they all had a different strategy and methodology – negative gearing, value-add projects, the land component having the growth, and so on. Which advice was I to follow? I could see that residential was less specialised and easier to 'get into' than the other asset classes, with easy access to equity, too.

I learnt to be both curious and sceptical about some of the younger 'gurus' at the time who had amassed large portfolios in short time frames. Some are mentors and reputable buyer's agents; others are sharks with their own agenda to just make money.

Knowledge empowered me to make good decisions, for myself and for my investors.

The more I learnt, the more I liked about using residential property as a vehicle for wealth creation. Here are some of the other key benefits:

- Everyone needs a roof over their head. This asset class is considered by most as a fundamental human right, alongside food, water, clothing and health care. Shelter will always be valued by people as a necessity, as opposed to shares, for example.
- Property is like a bricks-and-mortar bank account – it is tangible. As most people live in a residential property, they have a level of understanding of how the concept works, whether it's through paying rent or a mortgage. This is a great first step to be able to repeat the process.
- Residential is a secure type of investing because there is a physical object you can add value to.
- It is also less volatile than other investments, with tax benefits, reliable capital growth, long-term mindset, high demand and rental increases.
- Most residential properties in capital cities and regional hubs have quadrupled in value in the last 30 years.
- You can use other people's money – the bank's and tenants' – to finance your financial freedom.

On the flipside, it's also worth mentioning a few reasons why you shouldn't invest in property:

- to purely save on tax (especially overpaying for new or off-the-plan properties) while ignoring the fundamentals of property investment
- to buy property because of fear of missing out (FOMO) when the markets are performing well

- if you aren't financially fluent and don't understand how property works
- if your finances aren't in order (you need stable income and enough savings for a deposit).

If you want to better understand how property works, then strap yourself in and read on!

PART I
RESIDENTIAL VERSUS OTHER INVESTMENTS

eventy per cent of residential property in Australia is owner-occupied, and that is largely because buying property remains the 'Great Australian Dream'; as a measure of financial success, it continues to fuel the market. But with house prices sky-high, it's no longer the path to financial freedom and happiness – for many, it's out of reach. Luckily, there are plenty of other ways to make excellent returns through residential property investing aside from snapping up a quarter-acre block.

Let's take a look at some of the fundamentals of residential property investing. I'll go into detail about each point later in this book, but a brief rundown of how it works is shown in Table 1.

Table 1: The fundamentals of residential property

Deposit required	5–20%
Due diligence	Nominal
Yields	3–6% gross average
Leases	6–12 months
Bonds	1 month
Outgoings	Covered by owner
Repairs	Covered by owner
Depreciation	Average
Vacancy	1–2 weeks average (per year)
Cash flow	Neutral to negative
Loan interest rates	Variable over time
Capital growth	Market-dependent
Property management	Intensive
Value-adding	Renovations and developments (subdivision, townhouses, etc.)

Now, let's compare residential property investing to some popular alternatives.

Saving versus investing

Whether you're better off to save or invest will come down to a few factors, which are largely based on your appetite for risk. Regardless of what the residential property market is doing – it is always a popular water-cooler topic – you need to be comfortable and confident that your investing decisions feel right and are appropriate for your objectives.

There's a reason so many people who invest in property choose residential: it's more relatable, it's easier to understand, and just about everyone lives in a residential property. But what comes with that is the highly emotive nature of the residential property market. This is compounded by the daily media reports and coverage – it's easy to get swept away reading about other people's seemingly grand successes or failures.

The truth is that sometimes it makes better sense to save. No one could have predicted we would end up experiencing two years of a pandemic of epic proportions, and if you are risk-averse, combining this with another uncertain, volatile experience (which investing is) could just result in sleepless nights.

Yes, there is security in risk-off markets (low-risk investments) when the market is pessimistic about the economic outlook; so, if you believe that you'll need your money in the next year or two, it may make more sense to save. But think about this: when you put money in the bank nowadays, you usually *lose* money. This is because inflation erodes wealth, which is bad news for everyone except investors who park their investment money outside of financial institutions.

Here's something to consider: if the market crashes, you might think it's great to have cash again. However, it's likely that the

Federal Government will respond by inflating the currency, or pumping money back into the market to give it a boost.

Unfortunately, you are set to lose either way: you'll get left behind when assets boom, or your wealth will start eroding due to the increase in inflation. If the government inflates the currency, then the cash you have is worth less. Overseas goods – electronics, cars, travel – will cost more in relation, further lessening the worth of your cash savings. So, while it's great to have a cash buffer (say, 10 to 20 per cent of your total investments), holding cash is not a viable way to create wealth, in my opinion.

As an investor, in the worst-case scenario of the market crashing, you'd only lose money if you were in a position where you were forced to sell. However, by carefully structuring your purchases, keeping buffers in place and managing cash flow, you can ride out the bumps along the way.

The truth is that investing is a game of patience and should always be viewed as a longer-term proposition. The most successful property investors I work with choose to invest over the long term, and the longer your timeline generally, the better your investment outcomes. That's the best way to protect your portfolio from volatility.

And don't worry about trying to time the market, either – I am yet to meet a successful property investor who has sat on the side-lines waiting for a market crash!

Shares versus property

There's always a lot of noise around the share market versus the property market. The preference for one over the other never fails to fill column inches every weekend in all the newspapers and magazines, with industry experts keen to champion their chosen vehicle. What you need to remember is that, once again, whichever option you choose will come down to your risk profile.

The great advantage shares have is that you can set up today and start trading. Most of the banks these days offer a trade account (there are numerous online platforms) with everything you need to start buying and selling shares immediately. Better still, there are no ongoing commitments such as monthly repayments, lenders' fees or stamp duty.

When you're set up and ready to go, shares can outperform property on a percentage basis. This means that your returns may be better, and your portfolio may grow faster. Another advantage of investing in shares is that the process of selling is much cheaper than with property, so it's much easier to grow your portfolio. As a result, the share market is more liquid, with many bids and offers, and investors can enter and exit relatively easily.

However, the easier transaction process is a double-edged sword. Shares are more volatile, meaning that prices can fluctuate wildly over the course of the day – sometimes by as much as several hundred per cent. For investors who love the thrill of the market, this presents no problem: they accept that fluctuations occur in the short term but, generally, the value of their investments will steadily increase over the long term. However, it is a commonly known fact that most investors lose money in stocks (90 per cent is a frequently reported figure). Then there is the time element: they're happy to dedicate the time to checking their portfolio daily to see how their investments are travelling.

For those who prefer a measured and conservative approach, this can be challenging. It can be unsettling to feel your money is at the mercy of the market, and to see it increase and then decrease over the course of just one day. Furthermore, using leverage in shares can be disastrous. It may seem like a good idea at the time to take on more risk by dramatically increasing your returns, but you run the risk of losing a lot versus gaining only a little, which could put your portfolio in a particularly vulnerable position.

Property, on the other hand, can use leverage better than any other asset class. This is because the value of property often increases faster than you can physically save your cash, which makes it more efficient and lower risk. Because of its lower knowledge barrier – most people understand the basic process of buying and selling real estate – property can also be great as a set-and-forget option, if that's your investing objective. The tax benefits are excellent, and working with a great tax specialist will enable you to deduct many expenses you may not be aware of. Further to that, you can also outsource other elements of property investing to complementary specialists, such as buyer's agents, brokers and accountants. All you need to get started is a secure income, and you're on your way!

Cryptocurrency versus property

The cryptocurrency market has gained a lot of ground – and newspaper column inches – over the last few years, and I am often asked what I think about investing in crypto. It's not hard to see why, either. It seems there's no shortage of crypto funds, coins and investors who magically create incredible returns within short periods of times, and it's easy to be seduced.

Essentially, cryptocurrency is a digital payment system that doesn't rely on banks to facilitate the transactions. It's a peer-to-peer system that can enable anyone, anywhere, to send and receive payments. It is not controlled by any country or government.

Cryptocurrency received its name because it uses encryption to verify transactions. This means advanced coding is used for storing and transmitting cryptocurrency data between users' 'digital wallets' and to public ledgers (called 'blockchain'). The aim of encryption is to provide security and safety. Units of cryptocurrency are created through a process called 'mining', which involves using computer power to solve complicated mathematical problems that authorise transactions; in return, you receive coins as a reward.

Cryptocurrency can connect people locally and globally without the need of banks. For instance, around 57 per cent of people in Africa – around 95 million people – do not have a traditional bank account. This high number of unbanked people undoubtedly causes problems, as there are limited economic options for countries to serve their citizens, and more than 70 per cent of the payments and money transfers in these countries are fraud. Problems also arise in countries like Ukraine and Russia when international governments freeze assets. Cryptocurrency provides a way to transact and hold strong value somewhere.

The first cryptocurrency was Bitcoin, which was founded in 2009, and it remains the best known today. However, there are now thousands of other forms of cryptocurrency that have different purposes and uses.

However, like many things that are shiny, the lustre can wear off. What you need to remember is that as fast as 'hot' crypto deals pop up, they just as quickly disappear. Furthermore, the technology moves fast. For example, Bitcoin is quite volatile, and at the time of writing its value has halved over the last year.

Often the founders of some of the new coins vanish along with the promises they made to investors, or their ideas don't ever reach usability, which does nothing to create stability and trust in the industry.

If you're thinking of cutting a path through crypto, a good rule of thumb is to ask yourself two questions:

1. Do I understand why this coin exists and what it is being used to accomplish?
2. Do I think this idea can work consistently in the real world?

Adding further complexity is that cryptocurrencies don't have a way to be valued – so how do you know what you're investing in with confidence? When your money is tied up in an unregulated system, you need to be very comfortable with risk.

REITs versus property

REITs (real estate investment trusts) are organised partnerships, corporations, trusts or associations that invest together in income-producing real estate. A key benefit of REITs is greater diversification: you can invest in hundreds of properties in different property categories, such as offices, warehouses, hotels, residential property, shops and healthcare facilities.

REITs also offer relatively low risk: you are exposed to property without owning it yourself, and you can have the property professionally managed, which saves you time and effort in the long run. It also requires lower starting capital. With lower risk and lower debt, it's a fantastic option, particularly if you're looking at investing for your retirement. Its potentially higher total returns also make it a strong-performing asset class to consider. By owning, say, a 20 per cent share of the asset, you will receive the full benefits as the asset price increases (a five-times return on cash invested). This can be very appealing for investors.

However, one of the best parts about investing in real estate is being able to add value through renovation or developments, and you can't do that with REITs as you don't have control over the properties. Another great aspect of property investing that REITs don't offer is the opportunity to leverage your money. Also, it's worth keeping in mind that the price of your REIT can change regularly (although REITs are much less volatile than shares or cryptocurrency), which can be highly emotional for investors, especially during recessions. Furthermore, the quality of asset still matters – don't buy petrol station REITs, for example, as they will not be around for long after the implementation of electric vehicles. It's best to consult your expert team before you make any big decisions.

PART II
TYPES OF RESIDENTIAL PROPERTY

A quick scan along any residential street in most capital cities will reveal a multitude of housing types. Single-storey, double-storey, semi-detached, apartment – there are plenty of options and just as many price points, which makes for a fun weekend when you're out house hunting. However, this is when you must make a crucial distinction to avoid costly mistakes. You are house hunting with your property-investing hat on, not your principal-place-of-residence hat, which means that every decision you make must be unemotional. Success in investing is a clinical numbers game, and you need to be careful not to get swept up in the aesthetics of a property. Ignore the sweeping verandah and the Victorian fireplace, and instead investigate how the right type of property will yield investing success for your growing portfolio. With this in mind, let's work through the most common types of property that you should consider investing in.

CHAPTER ONE

STAND-ALONE HOUSE

A stand-alone house is just that – a freestanding house on its own block. In property investing, typically land value is the best contributor to properties increasing in value over time. The more land you have in a desirable location, generally the better the outcome. Given that stand-alone houses are on their own block, it stands to reason that they also offer the best land-to-house value ratio, and for that reason are the best performers for capital growth.

Another benefit of investing in stand-alone houses is that they don't attract strata fees that are passed on to you to pay regularly. Strata fees cover maintenance costs associated with a property in a building comprising multiple dwellings, such as an apartment block. They're also known as 'body corporate fees' or 'owners' corporation fees'. They cover things like maintenance of common areas and upkeep of gardens and amenities – the better the amenities, the higher the fees. As the owner of a stand-alone house, you won't have to worry about ongoing strata fees, as you are the sole owner.

A further benefit is full flexibility. If you buy a house, you have absolute freedom to do with it what you like, subject to local council approval. You can go all-in on a complete overhaul, or you may have bought a house that only requires a partial renovation. If you have a vision, your best bet is to buy a stand-alone house to give you the land space to make improvements. Land is your greatest asset for long-term growth, particularly in areas where population growth is confined, such as an oversaturated region or an area by the ocean, in the mountains or by a river – they can't make any more land!

The next step beyond renovating is to develop the land itself, again subject to approval. You could build a granny flat on the back or split the block into two with a dual-key. You could even build a series of townhouses or an apartment block.

It's worth keeping your end goal in mind. It's all well and good to refer back to my other book on commercial property investing and imagine life as a high-flying property mogul, but simply working with an existing house already on a good block will generally translate to strong results. This is due to demand – we love living in houses in Australia. There are also lots of tenants who have children or pets (or both) and will want a backyard, or who have growing families and relatives or guests requiring extra room.

Drawbacks

Because houses have more land, they attract higher price tags, which gives them a higher barrier to entry. With median property prices now past $1 million in some capital cities, it's harder to find a bargain than ever before, so this can add significant time to your investing plans – you may need to wait to increase your capital to buy, or wait to buy that unicorn property (which doesn't exist, by the way!).

Houses generally have lower rental yields than apartments but higher capital growth. As an investor, a high rental yield (the yearly rental income a property generates as a proportion of the property's purchase price) is desirable, and anything above 5 per cent is great because it offers stability. On the other hand, capital growth (the increase in the value of a property over time) is desirable too. Investors generally chase one or the other, because properties that have historically offered good capital growth tend to offer lower rental yield, and vice versa. However, there are still many regions where you can get both a high rental yield and high capital growth. Beyond the eight capital cities, Australia has close to 200 regional cities with a population between 10,000 and 600,000, and each of these will have their own supply and demand constraints at any given point in time, as well as differing economic conditions; however, some have historically offered both high rental yield and high capital growth.

As an investor in a stand-alone house, you have to cover all costs associated with the maintenance. Houses generally have higher maintenance costs, as well as higher insurance costs. You won't have access to a strata fund, as is the case with apartment buildings – the buck stops with you.

Finally, it's wise to put some thought into the tenants you will have in your stand-alone house. It goes without saying that this is crucial to ensuring your investment property will be looked after properly. For example, an older couple may sound great on paper, but they could have trouble maintaining the front and back gardens of your property due to mobility issues, so you might need to factor in regular gardening costs. If you choose a family with young children, you might expect some wear and tear on the property, which might require maintenance.

Summary

It's harder to find a bargain when buying a house, but they are the best performers for capital growth, so it's worth taking the time to find the right one.

CHAPTER TWO
TERRACE

A terrace property is a specific style of housing that dates from the Victorian or Edwardian era. These properties are usually found in the inner-city areas of major cities, particularly in Melbourne and Sydney, and they are full of character features such as timber floors, high and decorative ceilings, and fireplaces. They were designed in rows and share walls (which can make them dark inside); they have long hallways and often have their kitchen at the rear, which flows out to a courtyard garden. Many are double storey, too, with detailed iron lacework façades.

Terraces are usually well positioned close to the action of the city or inner-city suburbs, where restaurants, cafes and parks are also located. This makes them very popular with a younger demographic, who want to enjoy the social and lifestyle benefits available near the city. The heritage appeal of terrace houses is also attractive, and many have been restored or renovated with a 'box on the back' (a cheap extension that does not match the style of the original building) to allow for more space on their narrow blocks.

In terms of investing, these properties offer higher yields than stand-alone houses because there is more demand due to their inner-city location, which can equate to higher rents. There's also a greater land component than an apartment – and if you remember from the previous chapter, the more land you own, the better for capital growth – but with less maintenance required than a big backyard attached to a stand-alone house. This can work well with tenants who own pets, making them easier to rent out.

Terrace houses are also older (Victorian terraces started popping up in the 1850s), which can be perfect for value-add strategies. You might wish to renovate at the rear, subject to council approval, or update some of the features inside to preserve and celebrate the style, and also secure the future rental income over the longer term. It's worth noting that older terrace houses generally come with Torrens titles – meaning you own the land the property sits on (more on this in chapter 10) – while newer developments may be strata-titled, particularly if they have access to communal facilities.

Drawbacks

Due to their 'row' design, terrace houses don't have the same level of privacy as stand-alone houses. While most offer a double-brick construction, which adds significant insulation, they can still suffer noise issues from nearby neighbours simply due to closer proximity. This can be somewhat mitigated with smart material choices, such as noise-absorbing furnishings like carpets and curtains instead of tiles and blinds.

However, for those who don't like living close to others, the privacy issues will still exist, and this may preclude whole demographics that value their space. Typical tenants in terrace houses are transient – they may move for work, to grow a family of their own or, of course, to save and buy somewhere of their own.

Furthermore, newer terraces may come with strata fees, which means that you'll be expected to pay costs towards maintenance on a regular basis, as is the case with apartments. You might think you're buying a single dwelling, but you'll need to pay attention to the fine print.

Summary

Terraces are usually well positioned and can offer high yields, but they can come with privacy issues and potential strata fees.

CHAPTER THREE
SEMI-DETACHED

Semi-detached homes are a halfway point between terraces and stand-alone houses. You'll find these properties in inner-city areas as well as suburbs a little further out. They offer more space than a terrace yet still share a common wall with the next house, with the bonus that you'll typically only share one wall because the property comprises just two houses on the block.

Semi-detached properties offer a fantastic way to get a higher land value asset if you can't afford a stand-alone house, as well as a higher yield than a stand-alone house. They tend to exist on good-sized blocks and offer some heritage elements, such as timber floors, decorative ceilings and Art Deco detailing, with many built between the 1920s and early 1950s.

Due to their smaller footprint, there's less maintenance than with a house, yet there's more land area than with a townhouse or apartment. Outdoor space is also included at the front and back, which appeals to more buyers, especially those who value the opportunity to be outside with pets or children. There's more privacy too, with fewer close neighbours and less of a feeling of living on top of people in the inner city.

For investors, there can be opportunities to renovate older semi-detached properties to value-add, subject to council approval. These types of properties were very popular during the interwar period and, due to their heritage elements, offer excellent potential for renovating into their backyards or adding second storeys.

Drawbacks

One of the biggest drawbacks is that you don't have complete control of the property as you still have an adjoining wall. This can make future development problematic, as you'll need extra consultation and potential approvals.

Another drawback is that tenants and buyers may prefer to live in a stand-alone house for not that much higher cost or outlay in rent or purchase price. This may make it harder to find suitable tenants for your property.

Finally, tenants may wish to live in something larger, as semi-detached homes tend to be smaller than stand-alone houses.

Summary

Semi-detached houses are fantastic if you can't afford a stand-alone house on its own block, but you may not have the freedom to do as you please with it due to the connecting wall.

CHAPTER FOUR
DUPLEX

The duplex is a popular style today and has much in common with a semi-detached home. It is typically a modern-day semi-detached home. A duplex is two residential dwellings under one roof with a shared common wall. The pair of homes exists on one land title and can be owned and sold together or have separate titles and be individually owned and sold. The homes are separate, with two entrances and two sets of amenities, and often comprise two side-by-side, one- or two-storey residences.

A good way of looking at it is that you can own a property for slightly more than half the price of a house. In fact, they're a great way to secure a higher land value asset if you can't afford to buy a house. They're also usually higher yielding than a house, because if you own both residences, you can receive two rental incomes from the one asset. If you build a duplex, you can earn almost as much rental income as you would from two detached houses, without the extra land costs. Construction is also a lot cheaper as you only have one roof, one frame and one slab.

While each side offers less land than a stand-alone house, they offer more space than a townhouse or an apartment, which makes them easier to rent to people with pets and young families. There is more privacy as well, and a side-by-side duplex rather than a front-and-rear option means that there won't be tenants walking by bedrooms, which could impact privacy. Also, they are more modern than terrace and semi-detached houses, offering an appealing lock-up-and-leave lifestyle for tenants.

Finally, duplexes usually require a building insurance policy that covers both homes, but you won't incur the regular strata fees you get with an apartment.

Drawbacks

Duplexes tend to have been built recently and in a modern style, which can limit renovation potential, because they're already updated with good-quality fixtures, fittings and amenities. There also may not be the opportunity to renovate duplexes structurally, for the same reason – the builder or developer has probably already optimised the block, so there's nowhere to go.

Because duplexes tend to be newer and thus command higher rents than comparable older properties, tenants may also look around and see that they could live in an older stand-alone house for only a slightly higher price, which means they will look past your property. Plus, the smaller size of duplexes may lock out tenants seeking space.

Summary

A duplex is a great way to secure a higher land value asset plus a higher yield if you secure rent on both. However, you may not be able to renovate extensively and add value.

CHAPTER FIVE
DUAL-KEY

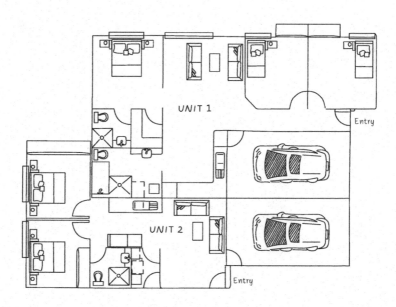

A dual-key property looks like a standard home from the outside but is divided into two separate units. A key difference between a dual-key property and a duplex is that dual-key homes have either one front entrance door and a side entrance door, or a foyer that leads to two different, lockable doors.

Both units are self-contained with their own bedroom, bathroom and living room, but they are not usually mirror images of each other, as is the case with a duplex. Often, a dual-key property is a house on one side with a unit on the other. A good way of conceptualising it is as a house with a physically attached granny flat.

In terms of investing, a dual-key property's biggest drawcard is that it offers two income sources. This means you collect the rent twice. As a result, the rental income will usually pay for all expenses, plus you'll have money left over.

Another big benefit is having only one council or body corporate fee. This is because a dual-key can't be strata-titled, so you'll only have to pay one set of costs, because councils view the construction as that of a normal house.

Finally, because these properties are newer in Australia, there can be tax benefits. For example, you might have the opportunity to depreciate some of the associated costs, which will help at tax time. Two bathrooms, two kitchens and double the fittings and fixtures could lead to higher depreciation. However, depreciation can be complicated, so you should always consult your adviser first.

Drawbacks

Keep in mind that you are going to be competing with all of the other property types to attract suitable tenants, and you may have to give up some time or cost in order to meet what the market wants. For example, if the property is older you may need to renovate. Dual-keys are typically only suitable for a small percentage of the rental market, such as students, who may not require the same level of amenity or size, and those who are willing to live closely under the same roof.

Also, your resale price may be lower because some buyers aren't interested living with tenants – and neither are some tenants, which could also lengthen the vacancy time.

Finally, some lenders may require a higher deposit, as their valuations do not typically match the purchase price. This is because they use normal properties as comparisons. Lenders may also change the loan serviceability requirements due to the increased risk of these types of properties.

Summary

Dual-key properties have the benefit of allowing you to collect the rent twice on the same property. However, they can be less attractive for tenants and buyers, which can hurt your bottom line.

CHAPTER SIX
TOWNHOUSE

You'll find townhouses in all the major capital cities; they're relatively easy to spot. Comprising an attached or freestanding property within a complex of three or more dwellings, townhouses provide a perfect, cheaper way to buy into a more expensive area, because you own a smaller footprint of land. Historically from the United

Kingdom, they were originally designed as the city option for those folk whose main – or larger – home was in the country.

Today, townhouses are popular because they're more affordable than stand-alone houses. Townhouses are also lower maintenance than houses on large blocks and therefore attract a range of tenants, from young professionals to couples, small families to retirees. Still great for families and those with pets, they have the benefit of an outdoor space – a courtyard or little garden – without the maintenance of a large backyard. The buyer owns the property but shares the land with a body corporate, with all owners sharing the responsibility for maintenance, insurance and upkeep in the form of a strata title. For example, you'll need to foot the bill for things like mowing the lawns and repainting the gutters.

As investments, townhouses have higher yields than houses (depending on strata), and there are government incentives if you're a first home buyer to purchase new or off-the-plan townhouses, which can be attractive.

Drawbacks

As a body corporate manages and maintains the common areas in strata-titled properties, and subsequently charges body corporate fees, this can eat away at yields. It's a good idea to investigate how much the fees are and how they are managed. Furthermore, any renovations you wish to carry out on your townhouse will need to be approved, especially if they will change the façade or the way it looks from the street. This can be restrictive and cause more trouble than it's worth!

On the other hand, if you bought off the plan, you are most likely buying at the peak of the market's value. As you're buying a new product, this leaves no extra room if the asset location doesn't perform the way you'd hoped.

Townhouses have also historically returned less capital growth than houses due to their smaller land component. It might suit to hold out for something larger so that you gain all the benefits of owning more land.

If you want to hold and sell later, you might run into problems with lower resale value or rental yields due to the competition from the other dwellings in your block. You don't want to be forced into lower prices because the place two doors down is cheaper, but you may have no other choice to be competitive.

Further to that, generally townhouses are in multiples – say, one of ten. This means you don't have scarcity of asset or a point of difference when it comes to searching for a tenant or selling. If everything looks the same, it's hard to stand out from a marketing perspective.

Summary

A townhouse offers great rental potential and is more affordable than other housing types, but you'll need to investigate the body corporate fees carefully.

CHAPTER SEVEN
VILLA

In some states, such as Queensland, the terms 'townhouse' and 'villa' are interchangeable. However, in others, such as Victoria and New South Wales, a villa is often considered a defined dwelling type: a small, single-level home within a small complex of dwellings.

Generally, villas are strata-titled (particularly if they have access to communal facilities), which means owners need to pay body corporate fees. However, some newer villa developments come with a Torrens title, which means – if you remember from chapter 2 – you own the land the property sits on.

Villas often appeal to an older demographic because they feature easy-to-access, single-storey designs that are ideal for people with mobility issues. Otherwise, they have similar benefits to townhouses: they're cheaper than stand-alone houses and offer higher yields (depending on strata), they're better than apartments for people with pets, and less upkeep (such as mowing the lawns or repainting the gutters) is required from the tenants.

Drawbacks

As with townhouses, a body corporate manages and maintains the common areas in strata-titled properties and subsequently charges body corporate fees, which can eat away at yields. It's a good idea to investigate how much the fees are and how they are managed. Also, if you want to carry out any major renovations, they may need to be approved by the body corporate. Proceed with caution!

When buying off the plan, you are buying at the peak of the market's value because you are buying a new product, which leaves you no extra room to make money if the asset location doesn't perform how you'd hoped. Villas have also historically returned less capital growth than houses due to their smaller land component.

Finally, another issue can be the lack of unique qualities in your villa. If they look like the other 16 in the block, you may be forced into lowering your price due to the comparable sales, which can make it harder if you wish to hold and sell later. Your rental yield can also be affected. A good way to avoid this is to look for any points of difference you can draw on later to use as a selling drawcard.

Summary

Villas are great because they're cheaper and more affordable to many tenants. However, villas have less land, which can reduce your capital growth opportunities.

CHAPTER EIGHT

APARTMENT/FLAT

Buying an apartment offers a huge amount of upside regardless of your tenants' age and lifestyle. There are millions of apartments all around Australia in all different places – by the ocean, in the mountains, in the city and in the country. They come in all sizes, too – from compact studios up to sprawling penthouses.

The big drawcard is that they offer a cheaper entry point and the opportunity to live in a location with higher land values. While maintenance, insurance and upkeep costs are shared in apartments among all the owners in the form of a strata title, they are generally a lot easier to manage and feature less depreciation as the exterior is managed by the body corporate.

Tenants aren't required to maintain certain aspects of the property, such as gardens and common areas, and so apartments are seen as very attractive to everyone from students to downsizing retirees. They also offer the ultimate lock-up-and-leave lifestyle, meaning that for people who enjoy travelling or have multiple homes, an apartment offers a very easy way to live.

Finally, apartments are generally close to the city, workplaces, parks and restaurants. You might also see apartments advertised with a 'walkability score'. This is a patented system that measures the walkability of any address using hundreds of walking routes to nearby amenities. Points are awarded based on the distance to amenities in each category; amenities within a five-minute walk are awarded maximum points. Properties with great walkability scores are relatively easy to lease, so these scores can be a great selling feature.

Finally, there are good government initiatives for first home buyers to buy new or off-the-plan apartments. There's also an overwhelming amount of research and information online about the benefits of buying a new apartment versus an old apartment.

Drawbacks

The most obvious drawback is that owning less land translates to lower capital growth returns. Generally, a sturdy apartment in an older 1970s lower-density building is a better investment than a shiny new compact apartment in a high-rise, simply because you would own a more significant equivalent land component per property.

There can be issues for tenants if the neighbours are noisy. It is inevitable than your tenants will have neighbours in close proximity due to the nature of apartment living, so if the neighbours are loud, it may cause problems that are out of your control.

Furthermore, some apartments have little to no outside space. During COVID-19 lockdowns, this made living conditions extremely tough for people in these situations. Having some form of open space – whether it's a courtyard, balcony or patio – will become even more important, particularly with working from home increasingly becoming the norm.

As with townhouses and villas, a body corporate manages and maintains the common areas in strata-titled properties. They charge body corporate fees, which can eat away at yields. Any major renovations to your property may also need to be approved by body corporate.

Furthermore, if your apartment is in an oversupplied area, you could suffer from lower rental yield, less capital growth and less demand as there's a larger selection for potential tenants to choose from. Yours will need to stand out, which is very hard to achieve if it's in a building of 200 that all look the same and have the same floorplan and fittings. Lenders also may require the apartment to be at least 45 square metres, so it's worth checking with your bank on their deal-breakers.

High-rise apartments have also been garnering a poor reputation lately, with cladding issues, structural problems, internet connection challenges and generally more complex (and expensive to solve) construction problems burdening owners and tenants alike. Some developers are in the game to make the highest return on investment (ROI) possible and produce bad-quality products.

It is generally best to stick with two- and three-bedroom apartments over one-bedroom apartments and studios. You will have a larger pool of tenants to rent or sell the property to; plus, one-bedroom apartments are generally limited to singles, so you may miss out on a lot of the market!

Finally, proceed with caution when buying off the plan. You're buying at the peak of the market's value because you're buying a new product, which leaves you no extra room to make money if the asset location doesn't perform how you hope.

Summary

Apartments are easy to manage and located in desirable locations, which makes them easier to rent. However, there may be expensive owners' corporation fees, and you'll need to pick your area carefully to ensure there aren't oversupply issues.

CHAPTER NINE

SPECIAL TYPES OF PROPERTY

There are also a few other property types beyond the usual suspects. They are best left to experienced investors, as they carry more risk and are generally less straightforward than a stock-standard off-the-plan or house on a block.

Boarding houses

In this special type of property, tenants have their own boarding house tenancy agreement with their landlord to rent a single room, or a sleeping area within a room they share with other tenants. Boarding houses are valuable because they provide affordable shared housing accommodation. They're most commonly used for short-term rentals: periods of three months or more.

These investment properties can return double (or sometimes more) the gross income for similarly priced residential real estate. Generally, the bank will let you borrow 70 per cent loan-to-value ratio (LVR) and accept 80 per cent of your proposed rental income when assessing your ability to make mortgage repayments. However, if the building was built for the purpose of being a boarding house, then the loan may fall under commercial lending, and you'll have to pay higher interest rates and a larger deposit.

These types of investment can be risky. They are often located in low socio-economic areas and attract tenants who earn low incomes or are otherwise experiencing long-term financial hardship, and are therefore at risk of missing payments. There may also be associated risks with potential damage to the property. In NSW, new boarding house developments are limited to 12 or fewer rooms. In other areas, the maximum number of rooms would depend on the floor-to-space ratio and height limits relevant to local council environmental plans.

Over-55s estates and retirement homes

This type of accommodation is provided for older or retired people. It's a very specialised asset class that is different to buying an apartment in a suburb, because rental retirement apartments are sold to investors to rent only to elderly tenants.

Generally, your options include independent living units (ILUs), over-55s villages and serviced apartments.

ILUs consist of detached or townhouse-style villas, or large two- and three-bedroom apartments. They're great for mobile, independent retirees set up for independent living and include universal design elements such as better security, emergency call buttons and larger fittings for greater access. They can range from basic through to luxury living. Over-55s villages are different to aged care because the latter involve a high level of daily care, rather than a much more independent lifestyle. Serviced apartments are smaller than ILUs and offer assistance for tenants who need a higher level of help with tasks such as shopping and housework.

In Australia, almost half of modern retirement communities are owned by corporations such as investment banks and large property companies, with the remainder owned by the private or 'not-for-profit' sector, including church groups and benevolent associations.

They operate under standard residential tenant agreements, with a specialist retirement village management company in charge on behalf of investors and an on-site manager (an employee of the management company) for day-to-day operations.

They don't perform well as investments due to the inability for rents to match the market: they need to be cognisant of the aged pension and rental assistance received by retirees, and are usually located in fringe suburban areas. Banks are hesitant to lend against these types of assets, too. But they do offer a low entry point to the market: the average price is around $140,000 to $160,000. Expect a gross yield between 2 and 9 per cent, minus the usual property-related expenses.

How do you find them? Your best bet is to approach the on-site manager of a community and have a chat with them about any potential opportunities.

Pros

- There's a growing demand for retirement accommodation.
- There are few options for retirees to rent accommodation.
- There's a lack of new supply and low-cost retirement accommodation.

Cons

- You have to dig deep to find them.
- There's not a lot of scope for secondary resale market.
- Every contract is completely different and has a complicated structure.
- Capital gains are constrained because of the inability to increase rent beyond the typical pension rate.
- Minimal capital growth opportunities exist due to lack of land component.
- There are no value-add opportunities.

CHAPTER TEN
TITLES

If you are looking at purchasing an investment property, you have to understand that they may have different titles. 'Title' is the legal term that refers to the ownership of the property. All property is sold with a title.

Contents

Because titles carry so much information, you should always perform a property title search on a property you are interested in so that there are no surprises down the track. Typically a title includes important detail about the property, including the following.

Ownership details

A certificate of title is the way to record and prove the official ownership of land. It's a legal document, like a passport or car registration, and there is one for every property in Australia.

Easements

An easement is an interest attached to a parcel of land that gives another landowner or a statutory authority a right to use a part of that land for a specified purpose. The easement is registered on the title of the property and affects a defined portion of the land; it is generally shown on the plan of the land with a brief description noted or more fully described in a further document. If you have an easement on your property, it may be difficult to navigate development applications or obtain approval for changes to the property.

Examples of easements include:

- rights of carriageway (rights of way) allowing the owner of landlocked property to access their land by travelling over a portion of neighbouring land – for example, a shared driveway used for a battle-axe block

- cross-easements, which give neighbouring properties reciprocal rights to use each other's property in the same manner – for example, for mutual support of a structure such as a party wall between terrace houses

- easements for services such as electricity, water or sewerage, which may be over or under the property and may run parallel at the rear or side of a property – for example, sewer pipes laid underneath the land by the local water authority, or an overhead electricity transmission line.

Mortgages

If there is a mortgage on the property, the bank holds the certificate of title, rather than the property owner. The institution providing the mortgage, usually a bank, will be listed on the title. If you're buying a property, it's important for the seller to discharge the mortgage before settlement or there could be significant delay. This is one of the jobs that the conveyancer or solicitor is responsible for (see chapter 28).

Covenants

Covenants were basically the first examples of zoning and are used to limit the way property owners can utilise their land. The wider meaning of the word 'covenant' is 'promise', but in the case of conveyancing and property the word is used to describe restrictions placed over land use. A covenant is essentially a rule or obligation imposed on the property title that you need to abide by as the title owner. Obligations can relate to big things such as how many dwellings can be built on a block or the permitted height of a dwelling, or unusual things such as keeping chickens on your property or hanging out the washing.

Caveats

A caveat is a type of statutory injunction preventing the registration of particular dealings with the property. The word caveat means 'beware', and lodging a caveat on a property warns anyone dealing with the property that someone has a priority interest in that property. The party who lodges a caveat is known as a caveator. There are two types of caveats: absolute and permissive. Absolute caveats do not allow any dealings to occur on that property until the caveat has been removed, whereas permissive caveats allow for dealings on the property if the caveator consents to the dealing.

Types of titles

There are several types of titles, depending on the property. In Australia, the most common type of property title is Torrens title, or 'freehold'. This means you're buying the land and the property (or just the land alone) and that the property belongs to the title owner – you. A Torrens title is legally binding and was first developed and named by Sir Robert Torrens in 1863 after more than 40,000 land grants vanished in the 1800s. Torrens titles are enforceable by law.

Following are the other common types of titles.

Strata

Strata title is usually a title for one of several units within the same construction. You might see a property referred to as 'strata-titled' or just 'strata'. It means that you own one apartment and everything within it, but everything outside your dwelling – such as communal grounds, gardens and facilities – is usually owned and maintained by the managing authority (the owners' corporation) and paid for through a maintenance fee.

Community

Community title is a little less well known. A good way to conceptualise it is that it's the halfway point between a Torrens title and a strata title: you own your parcel of the land, but you also own a section of what is deemed 'community' or 'common' property. This could be something as small as a garden bed, or as large as a driveway or swimming pool.

Company

Company title simply signifies that a company owns the title to the land. Buying shares in the corporation means that each shareholder is entitled to the exclusive use and occupation of a unit and shared use of any common property.

Less common titles

You'll also find less common titles such as Limited Torrens (where there aren't clear boundaries to the property), Leasehold (which applies to government-owned land leased for 99 years rather than being sold) and Old System (for properties existing before Torrens title, although these are hard to find).

Finding out about property titles

How do you find out about a property title? It depends on which state the property is in. Your conveyancer or solicitor can assist you. Table 2 provides a general guide.

Table 2: Finding out about property titles by state/territory

State/Territory	Platform
ACT	You can access property information at the Access Canberra website (accesscanberra.act.gov.au). However, to do searches and to access titles, you will need to visit a local Office of Regulatory Services or the Environment, Planning and Land Shopfront in Dickson. There's also an online subscription service option for a fee.
NSW	Various platforms exist, including Morris Hayes & Edgar (MHE), Direct Info, Hazlett's, LegalStream, GlobalX and SAI Global.
NT	No online title searches are available at this point, so head to a Land Titles Office or request a phone search. There is an online portal for professionals with a monthly subscription fee.
Qld	You can look up titles at qld.gov.au/environment/land/title for a small fee.
SA	Head to sailis.lssa.com.au, which allows you to search as a guest, without having an account. A small fee is payable for a property search.
Tas.	Head to www.thelist.tas.gov.au and pay a small fee, and you'll be able to do a straightforward search.
Vic.	Head to landata.vic.gov.au and pay a small fee to access easy-to-find information.
WA	Head to landgate.wa.gov.au and pay a small fee to do a property search.

PART III
THE NUMBERS

As with commercial property, residential property investment is all about the numbers and desirability. But with residential, there's also the intangible emotional factor that often gets in the way of good investment decisions. That's why it's so important when you're investing to look past the aesthetics and steer your eye towards objective measurements to determine whether a property is worth buying. In this part of the book, we'll look at the numbers you should analyse when you're considering an investment purchase:

- acquisition costs
- yields
- leases
- outgoings
- depreciation
- property value
- cash flow
- capital growth.

CHAPTER ELEVEN

ACQUISITION COSTS

Here are the typical costs associated with purchasing a property:

- deposit
- stamp duty
- lenders mortgage insurance (LMI)
- legal/conveyancing fees
- valuation costs
- body corporate inspection report
- building inspection
- pest inspection
- surveying.

I recommend you obtain pre-approvals and quotes on all services before proceeding with a purchase, as well as seeking advice from a property-investment-savvy, tax-qualified accountant (more about this in chapter 19).

Typical purchasing costs

Let's look at each of the typical purchasing costs in more detail.

Deposit

Most lenders offer 80 to 95 per cent LVR, so generally, you'll need a deposit of between 5 and 20 per cent. Once you've spoken with a mortgage broker or lender and know the deposit required, you'll then be able to work out your purchase price budget (assuming you meet the requirements to service the loan).

A simple 'back of the envelope' way to do this is to divide your available deposit by the lender's deposit requirements and add five per cent to cover items such as legal costs, inspections, valuations and government taxes. Your available deposit should not include your buffer for leftover savings.

For example, say you have $150,000 to spend and the lender requires a 20 per cent deposit. You also need to allow 5 per cent for acquisition costs, bringing the total up to 25 per cent. If $150,000 represents 25 per cent of the total, the maximum you can spend to buy a property will be $600,000. So, you should be looking at properties that cost less than $600,000.

Stamp duty

Stamp duty is a state or territory government tax on certain transactions, such as the sale of a motor vehicle, an insurance policy or real estate. Stamp duty on a property can also be known as 'land transfer duty'. The amount of the duty varies widely depending on the state or territory the property is in and the purchase price, and is subject to change by state and territory governments. Most commonly, it's a set fee plus a dollar amount per $100 over a certain threshold. It can also be complex to understand; however, there are many online calculators to help you estimate the expected stamp duty on your purchase.

Table 3 provides some examples of how it is calculated.

Table 3: How each state/territory calculates stamp duty

State/ Territory	Purchase price	Calculation method
ACT	<$200,000	$1.20 (or $0.68 for eligible owner-occupiers) per $100 or part thereof
	$500,001–$750,000	$11,400 (or $10,360 for eligible owner-occupiers) + $4.32 per $100 or part thereof over $500,000
	>$1,455,000	$4.54 per $100 of the total dutiable amount
NSW	<$15,000	$1.25 per $100 (minimum $10)
	$327,001–$1,089,000	$9,805 + $4.50 per $100 over $327,000
	>$1,089,000	$44,095 + $5.50 per $100 over $1,089,000
NT	<$525,000	$(0.06571441 \times V) + 15V$, where V is 0.1% of the property's value
	$525,001–$3,000,000	4.95% of the property's value
	$3,000,001–$5,000,000	5.75% of the property's value
	>$5,000,000	5.95% of the property's value
Qld	<$5,000	$0
	$75,001–$540,000	$1,050 + $3.50 for each $100 or part thereof over $75,000
	>$1,000,000	$38,025 + $5.75 for each $100 or part thereof over $1,000,000
SA	<$12,000	$1.00 per $100, or part of $100

State/ Territory	Purchase price	Calculation method
SA (cont.)	$100,001–$200,000	$2,830 + $4.00 per $100 or part thereof over $100,000
	>$500,000	$21,330 + $5.50 per $100 or part thereof over $500,000
Tas.	<$3,000	$50
	$75,001–$200,000	$1,560 + $3.50 per $100 or part thereof over $75,000
	>$725,000	$27,810 + $4.50 per $100 or part thereof over $725,000
Vic.	<$25,000	1.4% of the property's dutiable value
	$25,001–$130,000	$350 + 2.4% of the dutiable value in excess of $25,000
	$130,001–$440,000	$2,870 + 5% (or 6% for investors) of the dutiable value in excess of $130,000
	$440,001–$550,000	$18,370 (or $2,870 for investors) + 6% of the dutiable value in excess of $440,000
	$550,001–$960,000	$28,070 (or $2,870 for investors) + 6% of the dutiable value in excess of $550,000
	>$960,000	5.5% of the property's dutiable value
WA	<$80,000	$1.90 per $100 or part thereof
	$100,001–$250,000	$2,090 + $3.80 per $100 or part thereof over $100,000
	>$500,000	$19,665 + $5.15 per $100 or part thereof over $500,000

NB: All figures correct as of 28 June 2022.

LMI

Lenders mortgage insurance (LMI) is a fee that is added to your home loan if you borrow more than 80 per cent of your home's value. It is a fee that protects the lender – not you – should you run into difficulties with serviceability. The good news is that with LMI, even if you don't have a large deposit, you can still purchase the property and get into the market sooner. But if you hold out, then you must consider the opportunity cost of not jumping in sooner. It's worth investigating the lending market, because there are some lenders that waive LMI for certain professions, and government incentives that also waive it for first home buyers and are, at time of writing, backing loans up to 95 per cent with certain banks. In mid-2022's lending environment, 12 per cent deposit with LMI is considered the sweet spot between reducing your LMI fees and taking full advantage of leveraging; however, it always pays to do your homework!

LMI can be paid as a lump sum, although some lenders may let it be added to your loan amount and paid off with your loan repayments (in which case interest will be charged on the cost of the LMI). LMI payments, along with stamp duty, are tax-deductible as borrowing costs.

Legal or conveyancing fees

Legal or conveyancing fees are paid to your conveyancer or solicitor and include the cost of the searches they need to undertake for your purchase. What a conveyancer or solicitor charges for a purchase will usually range from $1,500 to $4,000, depending on the value of the property being purchased and the complexity of the deal. See more about conveyancing in chapter 28.

Valuation costs

Valuation costs can be incurred when you obtain finance from a lender, and lenders will only accept valuers who are on the list they've drawn up. A third-party property valuer can give a more accurate value for around $400 to $700, which is more than most lender valuation fees, but it could save you a lot of money long term.

Having said that, most lenders don't charge a valuation fee for applicants (although you may have to pay an application fee for the mortgage instead). Valuation fees typically range from $200 to $350; however, on more expensive houses, or in extremely rural areas, the fee can stretch out to at least $775.

Body corporate inspection report

If you're buying within a strata property, it's important to obtain a physical body corporate inspection report. This will identify any issues with the specific lot or common property and also notify you of any planned special levies to be imposed after settlement.

Building inspections

A building inspection is something you can't compromise on – it's one of the best ways to ensure you don't end up with a lemon. A building inspector will expertly analyse the property and detect any defects. An external inspector who hasn't been recommended by the selling agent is preferable, as they'll be unbiased. I recommend using an inspector who takes a lot of photos and provides descriptions of each item as opposed to using tick-box forms. If the building inspector is qualified for pest inspections, a pest inspection is usually performed at the same time.

Building inspections typically cost $350 to $800.

Pest inspections

As with building inspections, pest inspections are non-negotiable. You may be able to engage a building inspector who's also qualified to perform pest inspections and do both at once.

Pest inspections typically cost $200 to $500.

Surveying

A surveyor updates boundary lines and prepares sites for construction to avoid any future legal disputes over land and property boundaries. If no survey is supplied with the contract of sale, it's wise to have one done. Your solicitor or the selling agent should be able to give you a list of surveyors in the area.

Other fees

In addition to the fees already mentioned, there are usually some small miscellaneous fees such as registration, solicitor searches and bank fees.

Goods and Services Tax (GST)

There is no GST to pay or be paid on the sale and purchase of residential premises unless the property is being sold as a new property. The majority of residential properties sold in Australia are considered to be 'second-hand' and thus do not incur GST. It doesn't matter if the property is owner-occupied or an investment property, as the rule applies to all properties defined as residential and not new. However, vacant land is not defined as a residential premises, so if you're selling land, it may incur a GST charge – check with your tax agent.

First Home Owner Grant

The First Home Owner Grant (FHOG) is a national scheme introduced in 2000 to help more Australians into their first home, and may help you offset some of the costs detailed in this chapter. It's a one-off payment for eligible first home buyers who buy or build a residential property to live in. There are different payments depending on where you live, as shown in Table 4 (and again, this is subject to change by state and territory governments).

It is worth noting that you should select an asset based on its long-term fundamentals – be wary not to fall into the trap of saving $10,000 to $30,000 through the FHOG but then losing out on potential capital growth or cash flow.

Table 4: FHOG payments by state/territory

State/Territory	FHOG payments
ACT	FHOG has been replaced with the home buyer concession scheme, which provides a full stamp duty concession for eligible applicants
NSW	$10,000 for new homes up to $600,000, or up to $750,000 if you enter a contract to build or are an owner-builder
NT	$10,000 for new homes
Qld	$15,000 for buying or building a new home valued at up to $750,000
SA	$15,000 for new homes valued at up to $575,000 (if the property is intended as your principal place of residence and you intend to live there for 6 months within a year of settlement)
Tas.	$30,000 for new homes or off-the-plan properties
Vic.	$10,000 for urban homes and $20,000 for homes in regional Victoria, valued at up to $750,000
WA	$10,000 for new homes up to $750,000 that are purchased south of the 26th parallel (the circle of latitude that is 26 degrees south of the equator) and up to $1 million for new homes purchased north of the 26th parallel

CHAPTER TWELVE
YIELDS

With residential property, 'yield' refers to the yearly rental income a property generates as a proportion of the property's purchase price – the higher the rental return relative to the purchase price of the property, the higher the yield. It's a good idea to learn about how yields work, because property professionals and commentators regularly quote yields to express the strength of investment properties. Yields are calculated using the following metrics:

- **Gross income:** the total yearly income collected from the property. It includes rent and any other extras such as payment for electricity, water, rates, property management and other outgoings, if the tenant is paying these.

- **Net income:** gross rental income less all expenses, such as council rates, water rates, insurances, maintenance and property-management expenses. It's the amount the owner receives after all expenses have been paid. This excludes your mortgage repayments, however.

Understanding the yield of an investment is useful for comparing against results of a different type of investment, such as shares.

What is a good rental yield?

In metropolitan areas, especially state capitals, gross rental yields typically range from 3 to 5 per cent. Yields that are typically below 3 per cent are very high-end, luxurious properties. In regional areas, gross rental yield can be higher than 5 per cent.

There's always a lot of hype and commentary on yields, with many arguing that lower yielding properties are typically better for capital growth as they are in 'blue-chip' inner- to middle-ring capital city suburbs, whereas high-yield properties will have less capital growth but a higher cash flow. But this is not always the case! There are other factors – for example, higher yielding properties can have a higher chance of vacancy, or underlying vulnerabilities such as being in a flood-risk area.

There is a lot of data around which yields typically perform the best, however this is always going to be different in every market cycle depending on the type of property, the location and the demand for the properties. Choosing the right asset in the right location at the right time is the true art of investing!

How to improve rental yields

Look at the trend of vacancy rates. The vacancy rate essentially describes how much competition is in the market for rental properties. It provides a strong indicator of what demand there will be for an investment property and whether a certain locality will likely have difficulty finding tenants. A vacancy rate of 3 per cent is 'healthy' as it's considered the equilibrium point at which the market is evenly balanced between landlords and renters. As vacancy rates trend down towards 1.5 per cent and lower, the pendulum swings in the favour of the landlord. This means you will have a greater choice of potential tenants, and with the increase in demand for rental properties, asking rents will also increase.

Once you've chosen a property, there are a few ways you can increase the yield, which are all about enhancing the attractiveness of your property to tenants. Renovating will help you to achieve a much higher rent, and therefore yield, compared to the purchase price and renovation costs. This is a great option if you have an older house that has plenty of refurbishing potential. Here are some of the best ways to grow rental yield:

- **Increasing façade and kerb appeal:** Emotional tenants want to live somewhere they feel safe and are proud to be, and will pay extra to live in properties they deem to be well maintained and beautiful.

- **Better photography:** Investing in high-quality photography to market your property will bring more tenants through the door, and more applications.

- **Property staging:** This is where you engage a professional stylist to bring in furniture and soft furnishings to create emotional impact – and attract a higher price. See chapter 23 for more on property staging.

- **Adding off-street parking:** This is ideal for tenants with multiple cars who value safety.

- **Increasing storage:** If you have dead zones within the property, utilise them for storage. This could include an attic conversion, storage under stairs or creating new cupboard space. The more storage, the better.

- **Creating an outdoor entertaining room:** Turn a courtyard or part of a backyard into a new living space using clever design, which will add value for different demographics.

- **Landscaping:** You don't need to hire a landscape architect – even just adding in soft outdoor lighting is enough to create a mood and an emotional connection with tenants.

- **Allowing pets in the property:** This will enable you to attract a much wider tenant base.

- **Updating appliances:** Update the washing machines, dryer and air conditioners so that tenants have access to high-quality amenities within your property. They will also be easier for you to maintain long term.

Also, once you have a tenant in place, plan rent reviews. This will give you space to plan as well, but remember to seek market comparisons to ensure you are charging in line with what the market is willing to pay.

CHAPTER THIRTEEN

LEASES

A lease is an agreement that allows a tenant to live in a residential property in return for the payment of rent to the owner of the property. The lease will usually begin when both parties sign it, and once it's signed, the landlord and tenant usually can't end it without the other party's consent. A penalty amount – specified in a 'break clause' – will be due if the lease if broken.

For many investors, one of the hardest decisions is whether you should sell or lease a property. In my opinion, it's almost always worth leasing, because the tax benefits and the long-term compounding of the asset can be more profitable than selling. But you'll need to seek the right advice, of course.

What happens during the leasing process

Once you decide to lease your property, it needs to be cleaned and made ready for tenants. This may involve renovations or repairs on items so that the property is safe to live in. Once the property is ready for tenants, you'll need to research comparable leases in the area to find the right property rental value.

Then you can list the property. This is a task for your property manager, but there are also sites you can list with if you are managing the property yourself, such as rent.com.au. Hold inspections so tenants can view the property before agreeing to the lease. A property manager can organise to find a suitable applicant for you, with important factors to consider including current employment status, credit history and references.

Once you find a suitable tenant, they will need to sign the tenancy agreement. This should cover the size of the rental bond, the lease length and other specific conditions of the property.

You will also need to organise property insurance. Tenants can organise their own insurance for their contents, but you'll need to protect your asset with your own insurance for the building, as well as landlord insurance (covering loss of rental income, theft and damage to your property caused by your tenant). We'll look into this in more detail in chapter 14.

A lease on your residential property is a legally binding document. The items included on the lease include items (economic or physical) included in the rental price, built-in appliances such as stoves and dishwashers, any freestanding appliances such as refrigerators, washing machines, dryers or microwaves that you have chosen to include, and a break clause or agreed terms regarding either party cancelling the policy. The owner has the right to set forth the inclusions in a rental property lease as they see fit, but they cannot change their mind on the inclusions once the lease is in place unless agreed upon beforehand.

Types of lease

There are generally three types of leases, which will need to be negotiated with the tenant at the time of signing:

- **Short fixed-term lease:** an agreement that spans from a month to five years, required to be in written form. This is the most common type of residential lease.

- **Long-term fixed lease:** an agreement that exceeds five years, specifies that the landlord has the ability to increase rent and make modifications to the property, and includes additional clauses relating to closing the agreement.

- **Month-by-month lease:** an agreement that typically starts as a short-term lease, but after the term ends, the tenant can either sign a new lease or continue on a periodic tenancy. The tenant doesn't sign a new lease, but the terms and conditions of the tenancy agreement still apply on a month-to-month basis. Either the landlord or the tenant can terminate the periodic tenancy with one month's notice.

Generally, lease periods are for six months or one year. The tenancy (inclusions, price and so on) can be renegotiated at the end of the lease.

Vacating or ending a lease early

In the case of a tenant breaking the lease and vacating early, there are several associated costs that the tenant is responsible for and will need to pay. These include re-letting costs, advertising costs and compensation for loss of rent until a new tenant is found or until the end date of the agreement, whichever happens first. There are also the state- or territory-specific costs shown in Table 5.

Table 5: Lease-breaking costs by state/territory

State/Territory	Costs
ACT	Owners can include a fixed lease-breaking fee.
NSW	Owners can include a fixed lease-breaking fee.
NT	The owner can keep the tenant's deposit. Further costs can also be claimed from the tenant via the tenancy tribunal if the landlord's costs are higher than the amount of the security deposit.

State/Territory	Costs
Qld	Owners can include a fixed lease-breaking fee.
SA	The owner can charge re-letting costs, and the tenant has the right to ask about the re-letting process.
Tas.	Once the tenant has left the property (in the same condition it was in at the beginning of the tenancy) and returned the keys, the tenant is no longer responsible for cleaning or gardening issues.
Vic.	Owners can ask tenants to pay one month's rent for every full year remaining on the lease (up to a maximum of 6 months).
WA	Tenants are required to give a minimum of 21 days' written notice of their intention of breaking the lease.

Rent increases

Before a lease agreement comes to an end, most tenants are given the option to renew their lease agreement for a further lease term at an agreed increase or to vacate at the end of their lease period. You'll need to weigh up your options, too. For example, it may not be worth increasing the rent if you have ideal tenants, given that you could lose more than the rental increase by having a vacant property. If you do decide to increase the rent, the average annual increase is in the range of 3 and 5 per cent.

Rental increases are governed differently in different states and territories. In the Northern Territory, Queensland and Western Australia, rent cannot be increased more than once every six months; elsewhere it's every 12 months.

Why use a property manager?

Many savvy investors use a property manager to handle their leases and investment portfolios. A property manager takes care of properties that investors don't live nearby, or that they don't wish to manage due to the time and effort involved. It's important to mention that a property manager doesn't have anything to do with searching for properties, buying the property, tax or legal issues – they simply look after the properties once you own them by collecting the rent, organising the tenants and managing maintenance.

It's worth crunching the numbers when engaging a property manager. Some property managers charge a flat fee while others charge a commission (typically 6 to 12 per cent), so if you rent out a unit for $450 a week, you would lose $40.50 per week with a 9 per cent agent commission. That's $2,106 a year. This is covered in greater detail in chapter 24.

There are several benefits to using a property manager. First of all, outsourcing property management saves time and, importantly, the stress of 'human' interactions and issues. You'll also potentially attract higher-quality tenants because they are screened carefully by your property manager, and you'll avoid confrontations with tenants. Good property managers know how to keep their tenants happy, and your tenants will benefit from having someone to talk to right away. Your property manager will also enforce lease policies, chase up payments that aren't received, undertake timely inspections and negotiate rent increases. Plus, there are insurance advantages that come from hiring a property manager, and their fees and services are tax-deductible.

Security bonds

The security bond (or simply the 'bond') is a form of financial protection for the owner to cover any costs for which the tenant may be liable at the end of the tenancy, such as damage to the property, outstanding utility usage charges or unpaid rent. The conditions include that the bond will be held for the duration of the lease, and if the tenant fulfils the conditions of the lease, they will receive their bond back at the end of the lease. The bond amount must be specified in the lease agreement (generally 4 weeks' rent), and the owner can request additional bond in certain cases, such as when the tenants are bringing pets, or if the property is furnished.

Some states, such as New South Wales, provide a voluntary online rental bond service through Fair Trading that allows tenants and landlords to manage their bonds.

Alternative tenanting options

Most residential property investors rent out their properties to tenants for a standard lease period – say, 12 months. However, there are also other options available to investors outside this traditional path. Let's take a look.

Short-stay accommodation

Making your property available for short-stay accommodation such as Airbnb can be more lucrative than renting to a long-term tenant. You are also less dependent on your tenants – if you have a bad tenant, or if your tenant loses income, you won't have to deal with them for long. You can also maintain access to your property should you need it for periods of the year.

However, an Airbnb property is likely to be more labour-intensive to manage, because you need to ensure it is in tip-top shape all the time. The high turnover of tenants also means more wear and tear on the property, exacerbating this. These properties have higher expenses, such as for furniture, décor, appliances, amenities, TV subscriptions, wi-fi and utilities. You'll have higher rent when the property is tenanted, but you'll also have higher vacancy, so your income will be irregular; and Airbnb also takes 3 per cent from your earnings on top of this. Furthermore, legislation in this area is constantly increasing and changing.

You can secure specific property managers to organise the short-stay process in your property for you, including handling the booking process and arranging cleaning between stays. However, these managers do charge a percentage fee (typically 15 to 20 per cent of the rent), which can be higher than long-term rental manager fees. It is worth talking to them before you purchase a property you are planning to use for short-stay tenancies – they know the market in that area better than long-lease property managers.

National Disability Insurance Scheme

I am often asked about renting through the National Disability Insurance Scheme (NDIS), but I feel that this is an area that requires a considerable amount of experience and ability to successfully implement. Basically, this space requires next-level due diligence, and there are a number of salespeople already in this area who may not have your best interests at heart or fully understand the complexities of the NDIS.

The benefits of investing in NDIS residential property include higher-than-average rental income and rental security (the rent your tenant has qualified for is guaranteed by the Federal Government while they are your tenants). However, they have several drawbacks:

- They are harder to finance, with 20 to 30 per cent deposits generally required.
- They need to be compliant with Specialist Disability Accommodation (SDA) standards.
- They are indexed to inflation (via the consumer price index, or CPI) for the life of the scheme, whereas rents elsewhere may increase at a greater rate than inflation.
- They are specific-use properties, which generally have worse capital growth.
- Tenants can damage the property, and it's harder to make repairs due to limited funding. You also can't evict your tenants like tenants in an ordinary home.

- They tend to be new properties, and developers charge a premium when you buy a new property.
- The terms of the rental agreements are also fixed for ten years. This means that if you wish to sell, you must find an investor who will take on the lease (affecting the resale value).

National Rental Affordability Scheme

The National Rental Affordability Scheme (NRAS) is a long-term commitment by the Australian Government to investors prepared to build affordable rental housing. NRAS seeks to address the shortage of affordable rental housing by offering tax-free financial incentives to the business sector and community organisations to build and rent out dwellings to low- and moderate-income households at below-market rates (at least 20 per cent below the prevailing market rate) for ten years. It aims to increase the supply of new affordable rental housing, reduce rental costs for low- to moderate-income households, and encourage large-scale investment and innovative management of affordable housing.

The annual income-tax free incentive is $9,981 per dwelling at the time of writing, and this is indexed each year to the rental component of the CPI. It comprises an Australian Government contribution of $7,486 per dwelling per year (paid as a refundable tax offset or payment) and a state or territory government contribution of $2,495 per dwelling per year (in direct or in-kind financial support).

Potential participants in NRAS include financial institutions, investors, private developers, not-for-profit organisations and community housing providers who may build, own, finance or manage NRAS dwellings.

Drawbacks are similar to NDIS properties: they are indexed to inflation, they are specific-use properties, they can attract less desirable tenants, and the terms of the rental agreements are fixed for ten years, which affects resale value.

CHAPTER FOURTEEN

OUTGOINGS

Outgoings are expenses that a landlord incurs from owning a property. Depending on the terms of the lease, the owner or tenant can be responsible for paying them, and this can make a big difference to the owner's bottom line, because they must be accounted for. You can also outsource this payment to your property manager, which will save you considerable time and hassle. Let's look at some of the typical outgoings on a residential property.

Council rates

Council rates are a type of property tax that cover the cost of public or community services such as the running of the council, road construction and maintenance, bridges, kerbing, parks and gardens, council buildings such as libraries, community activities and advertising, tree and bush management, and pest eradication.

Local councils use property values to calculate how much each owner pays in rates – in other words, how much you pay will depend on the land value of your property. The council may estimate the 'unimproved value' of your land to calculate your rates. Unimproved land value is the dollar figure a block of land is deemed to be worth by the council without any buildings or structures on it. It's calculated based on its location and comparable vacant land sales.

Council rates are generally paid quarterly in advance. Some councils offer discounts for early payment, so it's worth checking. Exemptions from rates can apply to Crown land, land used for religious purposes, charitable land and land used for mining or forestry.

Water and utility rates

Water rates are paid to the authority that provides water and sewerage services to your property. The rates are generally paid quarterly in arrears and have two components: a fixed amount for providing the water mains to the property, and a variable amount based on your water usage. There's usually no discount for early payment.

Utility rates include electricity and gas, and they are usually separately metered. If the building has common areas that require electricity for lighting, for example, the strata manager will have a separate contract with an electricity provider and these fees are usually passed on to the tenant. There can be quite a cost variation among utility companies, so it pays to shop around. Most will offer a discount if you sign a longer agreement, too. The tenant is usually responsible for the property-specific utility rates.

Tenants can only be charged for all water consumption if the property is individually metered (or water is delivered by vehicle), the property is water efficient, and the tenancy agreement states the tenant must pay for water consumption.

Land tax

Land tax is a state-based tax that applies to investment properties in your portfolio, excluding your principal place of residence (PPOR). It applies when the total taxable value of the unimproved land you own is above the threshold for the Australian state or territory it is located in. The land tax threshold is reviewed yearly in each state and territory, and there are different thresholds for personal and company ownership structures. Land tax thresholds for each state and territory are shown in Table 6.

Table 6: Land tax thresholds by state/territory in 2022

State/Territory	Threshold
ACT	There is a fixed charge of $1,392 and no threshold.
NSW	The general threshold is $822,000, and the premium threshold is $5,026,000. The state tax exempts farmland and PPORs.
NT	There is no land tax.
Qld	The threshold is $600,000 for individuals and $350,000 for other entities.
SA	The threshold is $534,000.
Tas.	The threshold is $100,000.
Vic.	The threshold is $300,000 on the total value of all property owned by a person. PPORs, primary production land and land used by charities are exempt.
WA	The threshold is $300,000.

Land tax can apply to residential, commercial and vacant land. It applies regardless of whether income is earned from the land.

If you think the valuation of your land is not aligned with other properties in the area, you can lodge a complaint, as this could directly affect your land tax bill should you be over the threshold.

Property management fees

As mentioned in chapter 13 and detailed in chapter 24, property management fees are charged by a real estate property manager for managing the property. Property managers charge a flat fee or a commission (typically 6 to 12 per cent), so you'll need to choose carefully whether it's worth your time to manage the property yourself, or worth the investment to outsource it. In my opinion, it is better to outsource property management to free up your time for other money-creating investing activities.

Body corporate fees

A body corporate may be called an 'owners' corporation' or 'strata corporation' – depending on where you live – and is the entity that manages the common property of a building or complex. Body corporate fees cover everything from building insurance, to maintaining common areas, to shared utilities, to building works and repairs.

The funds the owners contribute each year to the body corporate or strata committee budget are generally divided between an administrative fund, which mainly covers day-to-day expenses, and a sinking fund (otherwise known as 'reserve fund' or 'capital works fund'), which pays for emergencies, capital works and irregular, large-scale works. Sometimes a special levy is required if unexpected costs arise that weren't considered when the administrative and sinking fund budgets were set.

Body corporate fees are calculated by adding the total amount required to maintain and manage the building for each year and dividing it among the owners depending on their proportion of ownership. The fees are agreed on at the annual general meeting (AGM), in which all owners in the building can vote.

Insurance fees

Insurance protects the owner's asset should something unexpected happen. The three main insurances required on a residential property are building insurance, contents insurance and landlord insurance.

Building insurance

Building insurance covers the physical building against damage. The property should be insured for as many items as are applicable to your area, including fire, flood, storm, earthquake, hail, bushfire and third-party damage. If the property is freestanding (that is, not attached to another building), it's imperative to have building insurance. In fact, most lenders will require you to have it before they'll agree to finance.

If the property is strata-titled, the body corporate will hold the building insurance for the common areas of the property – the shared areas. However, it's best to check what the body corporate insurance covers so you understand what you need to insure.

Contents insurance

For the contents within the building or dwelling in strata buildings, the tenant or occupier is responsible. Contents insurance covers the financial cost of repairing or replacing your household personal possessions and furnishings if they are damaged, lost or stolen. This can include your furniture, clothes, computer, fridge, television, tools and jewellery. If you own your home, you can bundle your contents insurance with your home insurance.

The tenant is responsible for their own personal belongings and items. If you lease a place furnished, however, you may want to obtain contents insurance yourself.

Landlord insurance

Landlord insurance covers the owner's loss of rent should the property become uninhabitable after damage caused by perils listed in the insurance agreement, including by a natural disaster. Rent cover isn't usually the responsibility of the tenant, so it's up to you, as the owner, whether you take this out. The decision will usually come down to your financial position and risk profile, and the risk on the property itself. Public liability insurance is usually covered in home and contents insurance, so it is worth checking the cover as you may become liable for damages to the tenant (for example, if a wall on your property falls down and crushes the tenant's work van).

Maintenance costs

All property types require general maintenance.

Owners are usually responsible for maintenance inside their premises, but the complex (if the home is not freestanding) will usually be looked after by the body corporate. Maintenance costs are often left out of real estate agents' presentations because they are usually for one-off items. Examples of maintenance costs include the following:

- repainting, decorating, replacing carpets, etc.
- maintaining landscaping
- servicing and repairing heating, ventilation and air conditioning (HVAC) systems
- performing pest control
- cleaning or painting common areas
- maintaining the pool
- urgent repairs:
  - burst water service or a serious water service leak
  - flooding or flood damage
  - broken toilets
  - roof leaks
  - gas leaks
  - electrical faults
  - storms or fire damage
  - a failure or breakdown of the gas, electricity or water supply (including stoves and hot water)
- larger outgoings or maintenance (infrequent):
  - boiler replacement
  - upgrades to kitchen and bathrooms
  - replacing decking, handrails, etc.

CHAPTER FIFTEEN
DEPRECIATION

Depreciation is the loss in a property's value over time because of ageing and wear and tear. One of the best aspects of residential property investing is that you can claim the property depreciation items as on-paper losses at tax time. Because you are receiving a tax benefit each year for the allowed portion of the loss, the Australian Taxation Office (ATO) may refund some of the tax you pay on other incomes. You can also use your depreciation schedule to adjust previous tax returns and claim back missed dollars. You can't claim depreciation on land itself, though, and its cost is not deductible.

Think smart and choose a good tax professional carefully, because they could save you thousands.

To assess how much depreciation you can claim, you can obtain a depreciation report from a quantity surveyor. Many reputable quantity surveying companies offer a money-back guarantee and fees that are 100 per cent tax-deductible.

When purchasing a property, it's advisable to have a quantity surveyor produce a tax depreciation schedule (TDS) as soon after settlement as possible. This will ensure the surveyor assesses the property in the exact condition you inherited it and will deliver the most accurate depreciation estimates. Then, it's essential to review and update your depreciation schedule if you do significant renovations. Each item in your property will have a specific depreciation percentage, which will be outlined in the schedule.

A good quantity surveyor will measure, document and photograph all qualifying items so you don't miss out on any deductions. In fact, they will probably find things you didn't even know were deductible. Also, most quantity surveyors won't charge you if there isn't an equivalent amount able to be depreciated against in the first year. You have nothing to lose by engaging one, and potentially thousands of dollars to gain.

A depreciation schedule includes a breakdown of all building allowance costs and all plant and equipment costs, the rates at which you can claim different items and the effective lifespan estimate of each item.

Calculating depreciation deductions

Depreciation deductions can be broken down into those for the building's structure (known as capital works) and those for plant and equipment. Let's go into these in more detail.

Capital works

'Capital works' refers to the building's structure and any items considered permanently fixed to the property, including the building itself and any structural improvements. Capital works can be written off over a longer period than other depreciating assets.

In Australia, the capital works deduction is available for buildings or extensions, alterations or improvements to buildings (including to leased buildings, such as shop fit-outs and leasehold improvements), structural improvements (such as sealed driveways, fences and retaining walls) and earthworks for environmental protection (such as embankments).

The deductions can also include:

- built-in kitchen cupboards
- doors, locks and door handles
- clothes lines
- bricks, mortar, walls, flooring and wiring
- driveways
- fences and retaining walls
- sinks, basins, baths and toilet bowls.

If it's not possible to determine the actual construction costs, you can get an estimate from a quantity surveyor or other independent, qualified person. Then you can claim a deduction for the full estimate in the year the cost is incurred.

Deduction rates of 2.5 per cent or 4 per cent apply depending on the date on which construction began, the type of capital works and how they're used. However, it's worth noting that even investors who buy properties built before the threshold dates are often able to claim capital works deductions on renovations to the property.

Plant and equipment

Plant and equipment are assets that the ATO deems easily removable, or those that are mechanical. They include:

- air conditioning units
- refrigerators
- ovens
- fans
- blinds and curtains
- carpets
- hot water systems, heaters, solar panels
- security systems
- light fittings
- swimming pool filtration and cleaning systems.

The depreciation of assets within a building is calculated on an individual basis in accordance with each asset's value and its longevity, which is determined by the ATO each year and referred to as an asset's 'effective life'.

Investors can claim depreciation on any assets they own within the property, but not on anything the tenant installed as part of their fit-out. It's worth noting that as the property owner and landlord, you can choose whether you provide some of these items and benefit from the depreciation, or whether you reduce your hassle and have the tenants provide these items themselves.

If the asset is worth less than $300, you can claim an immediate deduction in the income year when you bought it. If not, you use one of two methods to calculate an asset's annual depreciation:

1. **The diminishing value method:** This provides higher claims in the first few years and smaller claims later on, as the value of most items reduces this way.

2. **The prime cost method:** This provides equal tax deductions each year over the course of an asset's effective life. The prime cost method is also referred to as 'straight line' depreciation.

When you're considering whether to buy a property, ask the selling agent for the previous owner's depreciation schedule. This will give you an accurate indication of the added cash flow from depreciation. It's worth noting here, though, that you should never buy a property based solely on the tax benefits – the fundamentals of the purchase need to be sound!

CHAPTER SIXTEEN
PROPERTY VALUE

How is the value of a residential property established? There are few different factors that are considered.

Comparable sales

Valuers use a handful of recent comparable sales to give them a ballpark figure. The rest of the price valuation is dictated by the land and structure features listed later in this chapter.

There are also aspects you can't quantify that can affect the valuation, such as if the street commands a premium due to prestige, the property is near in-demand schools or public transport, or the property is of outstanding design quality.

Land

The land that the property sits on also contributes to its valuation. Valuers will take into account a wide range of factors, including:

- distance to:
  - the CBD or other employment opportunities
  - public transport

- lifestyle aspects (holiday homes offering remote working opportunities, closeness to beaches/mountains, etc.)
- shopping, entertainment and recreational activities
- scarcity (defined by how many people want to live in a particular suburb and how many properties are available)
- unique placement (such as on a busy street, near a golf course, or on the waterfront with access to a jetty or mooring)
- access to the property
- topography (such as if the property is on a slope with views)
- aspect
- square metreage.

Keep in mind that international buyers prefer locations closer to the CBD or other lifestyle attractions.

Structure

The structure of the residence itself also guides the property's value. Generally, properties that have strong kerb appeal and some architectural appeal can be valued more highly, but this will depend on factors such as the overall upkeep of the property and the building inspection reports. Generally, this valuation will cover the:

- type of home (such as a stand-alone house, duplex or townhouse)
- year built (and more broadly, whether it's old or new)
- build conditions
- building materials
- renovations that have occurred
- kerb appeal
- square metres of liveable space

- number of bedrooms and bathrooms (with more bedrooms and bathrooms increasing the property's worth, although these trends are very locally specific)
- fixtures and fittings
- energy efficiency (solar, etc.).

Economy and interest rates

The performance of the economy and its effect on interest rates can have a strong impact on a buyer's ability to afford the property. If interest rates increase, fewer people may be able to afford homes, which creates less demand. But there can also be less demand if the economy is flat, because confidence is also down and there are fewer people incentivised to buy. Governments have tools to curb inflation and house prices, and increasing or decreasing interest rates is one of the levers they use.

Government incentives (such as stamp duty and LMI concessions, and FHOGs) can also come into play to boost the market.

Remember, property investing is a long-term game; therefore, as you build your portfolio, you will experience times of lower and higher interest rates. Banks build a buffer into the amount they will lend to account for 'worst case' levels of interest rates. You should do your own stress testing, taking into consideration your own lifestyle expectations.

CHAPTER SEVENTEEN
CASH FLOW

Cash flow refers to the money that you either pay or receive as a result of an investment property. It is a measure over a certain time period, usually a week or a year. It considers the income from a property plus the monetary value of the tax benefits, and then subtracts the expenses. Cash flow is important because it will give you a clear idea of how much money you need to put into or will receive from a property each week. This will help you budget and work towards obtaining a passive income in the future (if you're not there already).

Things to consider when calculating your cash flow include:

- interest rates on the loan
- the rent return achieved
- the depreciation
- known outgoings
- an approximation of maintenance costs
- tax.

The tricky part about cash flow is that you can never know the cash flow for sure before you buy a property. Once you've bought, there are pre-tax and post-tax cash flows to consider, as depreciation and tax benefits may positively affect the result; however, you will need to budget for unexpected incidents such as emergency maintenance and vacancies. You can do some quick calculations based on the list on the previous page first to give you a reasonably accurate idea of your potential cash flow. If the cash flow is the income the property produces after all expenses, then the following applies:

Cash flow = (net income + tax/depreciation benefits)
– (mortgage repayments + all expenses to the owner)

Making your cash flow work for you

Investors will often choose between a cash flow property strategy or a capital growth property strategy, depending on their risk profile, their objectives and, of course, the numbers. A positive cash flow property (or positively geared property) is one that generates more income than expenses; positive cash flow is a good indicator that a rental property is profitable, and of how much money it may make.

If your goal is to retire on a passive income, you may focus on cash flow properties and acquire investment properties that deliver a strong return. Once you reach your desired passive cash flow per week, you can choose whether or not to stop working and live off your property income. It's a lot easier to live off cash flow than to sell down properties and live off the capital growth you have made.

Cash flow will help you build your portfolio. You'll need sufficient income as well, however, otherwise your serviceability will become an issue in getting property loans.

CHAPTER EIGHTEEN
CAPITAL GROWTH

Capital growth is simply an increase in the purchase value of the investment. You can achieve capital growth through the market doing the heavy lifting, or through different value-add strategies, which are covered in Part VII.

Historically, most properties in Australia have doubled in value every seven to ten years. Take the following formula:

20% deposit (leveraging at 80% LVR)
× capital growth (doubled value in 10 years)
= 500% ROI over 10 years

Generally, properties that appreciate in capital growth are located where demand outstrips supply. Think lifestyle, beaches and suburbs of capital cities and regional towns that are in demand but have a finite amount of stock. For example, in 30 years people will still want to be near the beach, creating more demand as population rises and driving up capital growth.

To some investors, an extra $150 a week in cash flow isn't as beneficial as growing their assets over 30 years, which is what good capital growth can deliver.

For now, it's worth mentioning that within the overall market cycle, the capital growth of different properties can vary a lot depending on demand for the property and its type, purpose and location. In any case, it's wise to have a long-term mindset when you're buying property due to the high entry and exit costs. Market fluctuations will occur, and for this reason profits made from property investments must be realised over the long-term. Adequate due diligence is essential for understanding and mitigating these risks according to your personal circumstances and expectations.

Factors that cause capital growth

The Australian housing market is a collection of around 15,000 individual suburbs, each representing its own unique market with its own unique set of dynamics. Let's look at the main factors that cause capital growth (or a decline in a market).

The economy

A strong or strengthening economy is fundamental for a rise in property prices. As the economy grows, demand increases. Residential property is less affected by economic volatility than other assets, however, as it is a lot more of a process to sell, and you cannot sell part of one – with property, as opposed to shares, you are all or nothing. Also, tenants will always need somewhere to live; therefore, the economy for residential property can't turn off quickly.

Interest rates and employment are two of the major factors that influence the economy, and these can change at both a countrywide level (for example, the inflation and labour shortage following the COVID-19 pandemic) and a local level (for example, the mining boom and subsequent downturn impacting the Perth housing market). Other economic factors that affect property values include:

- gross domestic product (GDP)
- wage growth

- unemployment rates
- household savings rates
- migration rates
- changes in taxes or tax rates
- changes in the overall population.

Interest rates

Lending interest rates can directly affect a property's price, as they will change the cash flow from the property and lower the costs to enter the market. A lower interest rate will increase the cash flow; hence, buyers will be willing to pay more for the same property.

History suggests that when interest rates fall, the median house price generally rises – but it doesn't always happen this way.

Conversely, when the Reserve Bank raises interest rates to manage inflation and slow the economy, the higher cost of money slows the rate of growth. At the same time, higher rates tend to reduce consumer spending, which can slow demand for property.

Rises in interest rates often correlate with inflation and increased cost of labour. This has the knock-on effect of making goods and services more expensive generally, including construction and maintenance.

Infrastructure spending

Infrastructure spending plays a huge role in the long-term prospects of a region.

The development of infrastructure, such as new freeways, can change the demand for property. Increased access to a region means cheap land and good roads, with resulting urban sprawl and an increasing population. This spurs yet more infrastructure spending, leading companies to move their warehousing facilities to the area and employ workers who may buy or rent in the area.

An area with an increasing population requires more services, and as the new region develops, more housing will need to be built to service the demand, along with other types of infrastructure including schools, train stations and retail amenities.

Population growth

Property prices are a product of supply and demand. Ultimately, what this means is that changes in population drive property prices. This may occur for a number of reasons, such as if the building of new homes does not keep up with population growth at a country level, if a particular location becomes famous or fashionable (such as Byron Bay) or as the result of a major infrastructural change (such as the extension of metro or train lines linking a location to the city centre). You can generally keep up with population growth figures by reviewing data from the Australian Bureau of Statistics (ABS) and local council resources.

Supply and demand

Capital growth is more likely to occur in areas that aren't able to be readily expanded. This is what you might see in some older inner-city locations, which have tight restrictions around development and are landlocked. With consistent on- and off-market demand and growth that doesn't peak and fall as often, coupled with rent returns that steadily rise, capital growth is more likely to flourish.

Once you understand these broad levers, you can use them to select your location to maximise your capital growth.

Location

Location is a vital factor in capital growth. The best locations are those where there is demand for owner-occupier and rental properties, strong projected population growth, good employment opportunities, lack of stock and a great lifestyle (which includes existing and future planned infrastructure). Great locations offer:

- health care
- schools and universities

- safety
- access to public transport
- recreation options
- lifestyle options and/or areas with natural beauty
- proximity to a major city
- diverse employment opportunities, with developments providing short-term opportunities
- growth drivers, which will drive rental return.

Land content

As mentioned previously, land value tends to appreciate over time, while buildings always depreciate over time. This makes land content very valuable.

However, land is a limited commodity, so you need to buy residential properties with a high proportion of land content. The best way to achieve this is to buy a stand-alone house, or sometimes a townhouse – but not a unit.

In my experience, most property investors get this part wrong. There are many spruikers out there selling the 'investment dream' of owing property in the form of apartments around Australia, but if you just think of this driver of capital growth alone – land content – hopefully you'll investigate the numbers much more closely and see that these types of investments can be fraught with danger. I'm not saying they won't grow, but historically you will make more from well-positioned land content.

Timing

There are two schools of thought on timing. First, you'll often hear from people in your network waiting for the 'right time' to buy or sell. But if you keep waiting for the best time to invest in real estate, you'll miss it, because the reality is that the best time to buy is *when you are ready*.

Second, property growth usually happens in cycles, so if you do know what you are doing and you understand the cycles, it's important to invest in the right markets at the right time. There are plenty of experts who will tell you that you should never buy in a boom and only invest during a downturn or recovery period in the property cycle; generally, 40 to 70 per cent of market's growth occurs in a two- to three-year window.

Further to this, different markets cycle at different times. If you're building a portfolio of properties, it pays to invest in different markets so you can diversify your portfolio and make the most of the different cycles.

In investment terms, time is your friend. Compound growth magnifies a return over time. My advice is to hold onto your investments for as long as you can, because the longer you hold your property, the more it will grow in value.

Individual property factors

The specific attributes of a property can also, of course, determine its value. Key points such as the age of the building and its services can influence demand, and if the property has development potential or the council zoning changes, this can instantly affect its value. Properties that are zoned from low-density to a higher density instantly increase in value, as they gain developer appeal.

The market cycle

Let's examine the different phases of capital growth in the market cycle in a bit more detail. Figure 1, over the page, illustrates the typical cycle of the property market, with recovery, boom, slowdown and recession phases.

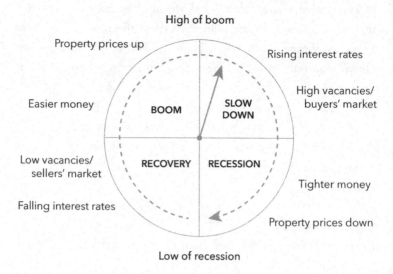

Figure 1: The property market cycle

High of boom

Property prices up

Rising interest rates

Easier money

High vacancies/
buyers' market

BOOM

SLOW
DOWN

Low vacancies/
sellers' market

RECOVERY

RECESSION

Falling interest rates

Tighter money

Property prices down

Low of recession

Recovery

The recovery phase is characterised by high vacancies and no new construction. Occupancy levels are near or at their low, and rental rate growth is either negative or flat, as owners offer rent concessions to avoid the occupancy rate falling further. As the population grows or market conditions improve, vacancy rates will tighten, and the market will begin to grow again.

The most successful investors understand that property investing is a long-term game – you could be looking at the best part of 30 to 50 years with multiple property cycles. Strap yourself in! Yes, it's possible to pick up a bargain-priced property during the recovery phase and hold it for two to four years until the boom phase. If so, it's best to buy a fundamentally solid property in a great location and capitalise when rents increase, and it may be wise to look at refinancing the property in the next phase to extract equity if you're looking to grow the portfolio.

Boom

A boom or expansion phase is characterised by falling vacancies and increased buyer demand. Demand pushes up rent and property prices, leading developers to start building properties; the most capital growth occurs in this phase. This is typically a seller's market, but buyers may be able to profit from the climbing market by purchasing properties with current deficiencies at a discount and repositioning them to sell on or refinance. Some common examples of this include finding rundown properties, and renovating or buying development or subdivision projects.

Growth in GDP is usually back at normal levels. At the high point of the boom curve, supply and demand are evenly matched. When developers release their new stock, there'll be more movement among tenants as they seek more competitive rents.

Slowdown

The slowdown phase is characterised by an increase in new construction and slow increases in vacancy rates as developers' new constructions come onto the market, leading to oversupply. The rise in vacancies can also be due to a pullback in demand caused by a shift in the economy.

Rents continue to rise, but more slowly. This becomes a buyer's market, as there's more stock available than is being bought. As more properties are listed online and more 'For lease' and 'For sale' signs go up in an area, rents begin to fall. Some investors decide to sell during this phase because of the risk of a recession.

Recession

In a recession, vacancy rates rise substantially as yet more new properties hit the market. Landlords offer rent concessions to try to retain tenants, causing rents to become more competitive. Developers who are late to the game will start offloading stock at below-market prices before the recession really hits. As the supply becomes saturated, prices will stagnate for a while, and rent growth will be negative or below the rate of inflation.

This is a great time for investors to buy at highly discounted rates, with the aim of holding the property longer term and waiting for the next boom.

The cycle of market emotions

Emotion plays a huge role in the real estate industry and can be responsible for huge swings in market growth or decline. When optimism, excitement, fear, panic and hope are involved, booms and recessions can occur with no real economic stimulation. Humans generally act with a herd mentality, which can snowball these effects. Similar to the market cycle, these emotions can be location-based or asset-type-based. This is illustrated in Figure 2.

Figure 2: The cycle of market emotions

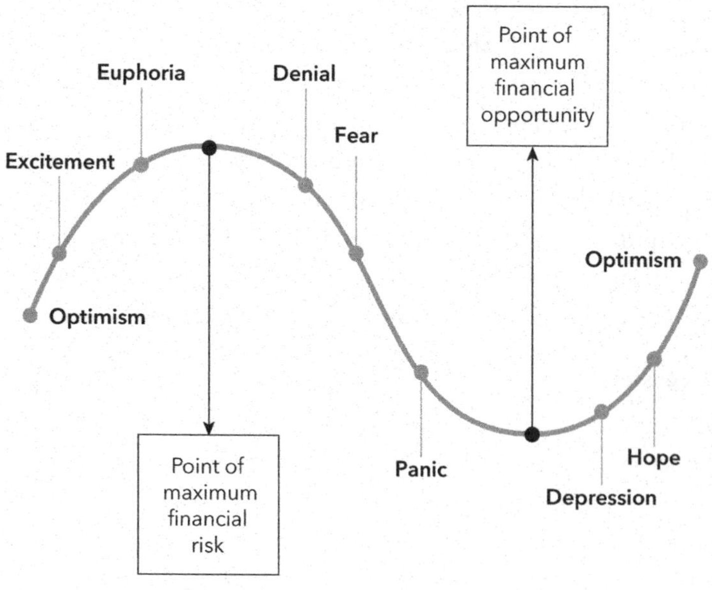

During a rise in property prices, optimism and excitement build. As the cycle approaches its peak, emotions are at the highest point, as most people in the market are making money and there are a lot of buyers. This is a seller's market; the buyers will generally lose out in the coming years.

As prices begin to fall, many buyers who have ridden the wave start to feel anxious; as the market continues to drop, fear increases, and some owners will look to sell to minimise their losses. This becomes a buyer's market, with more buyers than sellers. When property prices approach the bottom of the cycle, there is even more fear, and the doom and gloom will be reflected in media reports.

Many buyers and sellers rely on the way the share market functions to guide them when buying or selling a property – if they think the share market will go down, they buy property, whereas if they think shares are going up they will focus on the share market and buy property with the profits. This approach normally instils fear in the buyer, rather than confidence, and can be a trigger for some of the cycle of market emotions. A 5- to 20-year approach should be taken, no matter what market you are in, and you should assess the current and long-term risks.

Eventually, however, the market will begin to rise, and optimism and excitement will re-emerge.

Is it worth mentioning that while this model is useful to understand, Australia did not experience a countrywide recession between 1991 and 2020 – so, for 29 years! This is why due diligence is important and locality plays such an important role in the prosperity of a property.

PART IV
BUYING AND SELLING PROPERTIES

Part III covered the numbers you need to run in order to be able to assess a property investment and make a plan for expanding your portfolio and achieving your goals. Now, let's look broadly at the steps involved in buying and selling residential properties, including:

- preparation
- searching for properties
- choosing new versus old properties
- the acquisition process
- selling and exit strategies
- property management.

CHAPTER NINETEEN
PREPARATION

So, you've decided property is right for you. You understand the different types and the numbers used to analyse property investments, and you want to get started. If it all seems overwhelming, I've broken it down to six useful preparation steps. It's also handy to keep in mind that you can apply these steps regardless of what type of property you are buying:

1. Assess your current financial position.
2. Work out your purchase price range.
3. Decide whether you're a passive or active investor.
4. Set some goals.
5. Develop a plan.
6. Build your team.

Buying property and building a portfolio is not for the faint-hearted. Once you've worked through these six preparation steps, you should be ready to move into actually buying and selling property.

1. Assess your current financial position

First, you need to know your current financial position:

- **Cash on hand:** How much cash do you have to invest? What is your usable equity? Do you understand valuations? A key part of becoming financially literate is being aware of how usable equity works, as opposed to the gross equity in your home or investment property. Equity is the difference between the value of your home and how much you owe on it. As the name would suggest, usable equity is the equity that you can actually access, which is lower than your total home equity. This is usually equivalent to 80 per cent (or allowable LVR) of your property's value minus the remaining balance on your mortgage.

- **Income:** What is your income? How stable is your employment? What is the longevity of your paid employment?

- **Cash flow:** Analyse your present cash flow from your assets – property, cash, shares, businesses, superannuation and so on – and compare this to your liabilities. Do you have property or business loans? Car loans? Credit cards or personal loans? What are your financial family commitments?

- **Borrowing capacity:** Speak with a broker or lender to find out how much you can borrow.

- **Credit rating:** Find out your credit rating. In Australia, there are three reporting agencies from which you can obtain your credit rating report: Equifax, illion and Experian.

- **Your risk profile:** Analyse your risk profile, how much buffer would be required and how much financial stress you can handle. A financial adviser can help with this.

2. Work out your purchase price range

The second step is to work out what sort of price you're able to pay for a property based on your current financial position. Speaking with a broker or lender can give you an indication based on your personal circumstances.

If you have a surplus of cash, it may be possible to look at properties that require immediate renovations so you can achieve a quick equity gain and reinvest.

If money is tight, a lower-priced tenanted property that is cash-flow positive from the start may be better than waiting for a higher-priced one. Buying two cheaper properties over time would have the benefit of diversifying your asset types and their locations, as well as having two tenants. Weigh up whether it's better to buy one or two cheaper properties now or wait until you can afford a more expensive one that may be of higher quality.

In the long run, higher-quality assets could compound at a larger percentage with less price volatility in tough times, because of high demand for the asset.

What you choose will depend on how quickly you can save more money, as sometimes getting into the market sooner has a better net result than waiting and saving, since you could be missing out on capital growth, which may be more than your rate of saving (opportunity cost).

3. Decide whether you're a passive or active investor

Next, think about whether you'd be best as a passive or an active investor. A passive investor wants the property to perform as well as possible with a minimal investment of time, whereas an active investor has the time and the inclination to be closely involved in searching for a property and adding value to it.

To help you work out which investor type you will be, you need to know where your time is best spent – for example, working for an income or in a business startup – and how much time you have available in a day. If you've decided you're an active investor but don't have enough time to devote to the process, engaging a buyer's agent could be a good option. My clients engage me to do the legwork for them: researching properties, running the numbers and then presenting them with different purchase options. We'll discuss buyer's agents further in step 6: 'Build your team'. Active investing may protect you if your chosen suburb underperforms, as you can fabricate a profit through value-add techniques.

4. Set some goals

As I've mentioned before, your goals will depend on where you are in your life, your risk profile, how aggressive you want to be, and what you want to achieve (portfolio size, cash flow and so on) and over what time frame. Also, remember that your goals cannot be only about the money – what will make you happy while you're building wealth and after you achieve the level of wealth you'd like? As I mentioned earlier, for me it's travelling, meeting up with friends, mountaineering, feeling appreciated and working on passion projects that float my boat.

You need to envisage the long term and plan for it, but there are so many life variables that the long term is hard to predict. So, you need realistic short- and medium-term goals – focusing on these will give you the best chance of achieving your long-term goals. Write down your goals, be flexible along the way, and reward yourself as you reach each milestone. A buyer's agent or financial adviser will be able to assist you with setting these goals.

A big reason why many people never start investing in residential property is that it seems overwhelming, and so they don't take action. They feel that success in investing is unattainable; but there are very doable ways to achieve the life you seek. This is why goal setting and developing a plan are so important.

5. Develop a plan

Developing your own plan is about looking at the numbers required to reach your goals, then working backwards from there. It can be helpful to consult a financial adviser at this point to draw on their experience and knowledge and ensure your plan is achievable. We'll see how this looks in chapter 33 with an example 15-year plan.

6. Build your team

Purchasing property isn't something you can or should do solo; choose a team of trusted individuals to assist you through the process. There are multiple ways to find your team, with referrals and online searches being the most common. However, one of the better methods is to find successful investors and ask them who they use. Very successful investors have strong teams they can trust. When vetting individuals and teams, look at their qualifications, of course, but also consider the following questions:

- Do you like them? This is very important, as is the reverse – because if they like you, they're more likely to work harder for you.
- Do they sound competent and confident? Check out their websites and reviews.
- What is their experience? Have they been in the business long? Do they have the skillset for your particular investment?
- Do you feel you can trust them? Assess what personal benefit they'll get from your business.
- Do they have good communication skills, and do you feel they'll deliver when they say they will?
- Do they fit your risk temperament? Ask questions about their own appetite for risk and see how closely this aligns with your own.
- Do you fundamentally agree with their investment thesis? You have to be confident in what they are buying on your behalf.

If you can, try to speak with their previous clients, who'll usually be happy to share their views. It is important to understand how the agent is different to their competitors. You can ask them to provide the details of some previous clients to discuss this.

A great finance broker or bank manager, accountant, buyer's agent, conveyancer or solicitor, property manager, town planner and valuer are worth their fees many times over. A mentor of some kind (paid or unpaid) can also be invaluable.

Let's look now at what each of these advisers does and why you may need them.

Finance broker or bank manager

Number one on the list is a finance broker or bank manager, because they organise the finance aspect of the process and you can't do the deal without them. But you need a finance broker or bank manager who has extensive experience in lending. This is because someone experienced will ensure you get the best rate and lender for your situation, as there are lenders who may be able to finance you when the major lenders will not. Most brokers will get paid directly by the lender and will generally get paid the same by all lenders, so they can do all the work for you looking at all the lenders and finding you the best deal – it's worth speaking with one.

It's important to be aware of how your broker charges. Some brokers can charge an upfront commission as a percentage of the total value of the loan – so the larger the loan, the greater the pay-off for the broker. This can work well – as investors, we want to leverage as much as we can, so our incentives are aligned; however, be wary of a broker recommending a larger loan than you've budgeted for. Other brokers can charge a trail commission as a percentage of the mortgage that they continue to receive over the life of the loan. The issue with trail commissions is that brokers have no obligation to provide any service to you during the life of the loan; and the less ongoing work brokers do, the better it is for them, because they're getting paid for doing nothing. Plenty of buyers get caught out over this.

There are some great ways you can get peace of mind with your broker decision. A broker is legally required to provide you with a document called a 'credit guide', which provides their contact details and a record of the commission they will earn if you go ahead with the loan, so you can follow the money trail; make sure you get a copy. Ask about their lending panel – finance brokers are restricted as to what banks they can access. And ask who owns them – some brokers are franchise owners or part-owned by big banks, so it's important that you understand where their money is coming from.

Make sure your broker can articulate the choices in plain English. There are many types of loans on the market, and it can be confusing – your broker should present you with a number of options and clearly explain their reasons for recommending specific loans.

Be wary of brokers who aren't focused on getting the best mortgage deal for you. A good broker will be able to tell you the shortcomings of different deals – such as the break costs of a lower-interest-rate deal – and why and when to avoid these depending on your strategy. A mediocre broker will just chase the best interest rate with the least amount of effort on their part. They should focus on your agenda, not theirs. Be wary, too, of brokers who try to upsell you tangentially related products such as life insurance.

Remember that property finance methodology can be just as important as property selection methodology. It's crucial to get this right.

Accountant

It is essential to find an accountant who has experience with large-portfolio clients and who understands the big picture aligned with your property wealth creation strategy. They will be able to tell you which structure is best for buying each property, depending on its purpose and cash flow. Please note, though, that accountants aren't financial advisers, so investment advice outside the realm of tax should be questioned, as they may have ulterior motives.

While it may be hard to tell straight off the bat, it's invaluable to find an accountant who is proactive. They will update you with new opportunities (such as when laws change or are updated) and demonstrate that they are active partners with you over the long term, not just for one transaction.

For example, many accountants will advocate for you to buy a negatively geared property simply to save tax, and will recommend an off-the-plan property for tax savings. Their advice can run counter to growing a portfolio because they are generally deductions-focused, while an investor wants to increase their income to borrow more. You need to find that sweet spot and balance, and recognise that your accountant must be property-investment-focused, or else they may potentially be working against you.

An accountant is also a great source of advice. They can provide guidance on how to structure your purchase, which can be incredibly important long term. For example, if you only want to hold the property for 5 to 10 years as opposed to 20 or 30, they can determine whether you should buy in your personal name or in that of a trust or company. Also, if you plan to be more active and potentially develop this property at a later date, structuring and asset protection is extremely important.

Furthermore, a good accountant will disagree with you and be able to clearly illustrate the best way to do things. After all, you're paying them for their years of experience. If you're not happy, be confident to leave them and change.

Mentor

It's always great to have someone to discuss each property deal with – whether that's someone highly experienced, an online forum, or a paid adviser such as a buyer's agent. Just make sure that the person you choose as a mentor has bought many properties outside of where they live, so they truly have in-depth knowledge of property investing. Remember to select someone who has the capability to understand your particular needs and an ethos that aligns with your goals and strategy. In other words, don't approach someone aggressive and high risk if you are a set-and-forget, low-risk buyer. Remember to only take advice from someone who is where you want to be.

Buyer's agent

Buyer's agents are the opposite of selling agents: they represent the buyer. They can handle the whole research and purchasing process for you, which is very advantageous for any investor, and particularly if you're inexperienced, nervous or time poor. A buyer's agent's service includes:

- sales and data research
- due diligence
- recommending building and pest inspectors, conveyancers and property managers
- negotiation of property purchases
- supporting you through the purchasing process.

A buyer's agent will also often have access to off-market properties. As a buyer's agent myself, of course I think we are well worth our fee. You'll learn from our expertise, see more quality properties, save time and be able to negotiate a better price with selling agents.

When seeking the support of a buyer's agent, services can be tailored to your needs – whether that means handholding for a first purchase or reshuffling a large portfolio to reinvest the equity built up. An experienced buyer's agent will have navigated the highs and lows of hundreds – if not thousands – of purchases. They will know what common mistakes to avoid and when to be punchy on getting a deal done.

Buyer's agents work on a commission basis paid by you, but be aware that they have minimal liability if they buy you a poor-quality property – so it's critical that you find an ethical agent who has many positive reviews and proven results.

Be wary of buyer's agents who you do not pay. If you are not paying them, then someone else is, which means they may not have your best interests at heart.

A lot of investors end up buying in their backyard because they feel comfortable that they understand the area, and they don't consider buying interstate. There are thousands of markets within Australia, all with different growth drivers and at different stages of their property cycles. Engaging an experienced buyer's agent with an in-depth knowledge of an interstate market you may not have purchased in on your own could really fast-track and grow your portfolio.

Conveyancer/solicitor

Some conveyancers and solicitors are generalists, while others are experts in one particular area of law. It's crucial that you engage a highly competent property solicitor who is experienced in property acquisition, leasing and due diligence. There are even solicitors who specialise in each of these fields.

It's also imperative that they have a hands-on approach and don't pass your purchase on to be handled by a paralegal or support staff. Don't just choose the cheapest conveyancer or solicitor you can find – buying a property is a major investment, and it's important to have the right person on your team. So, before you engage someone, ask them how many deals they've done and if they can provide any references. Again, online reviews can assist as a starting point in your search.

Note that if you're buying in different states, it's usually best to use a solicitor from the state the property is in, or even the same region or town, because they'll have more local knowledge.

More details about conveyancing are provided in chapter 28.

Property manager

Local property managers are another great source of information. They'll be able to quickly give you the typical vacancy periods of similar properties to those you're looking at. Property managers are a fountain of knowledge about the market because they live and breathe property. They know who wants to lease in the area, who is looking to buy, and information about the demographic for the future.

Property managers also have excellent networks, including tradespeople they can recommend. This alone can be invaluable to save you googling for someone to fix your investment property's plumbing. Their contacts will most likely be able to access cheaper rates, too, due to the repeat work from the manager across other properties.

As your trust grows with the property manager, you can give them permission to manage bills, sign off maintenance repairs up to a specified value and be the contact for insurers in the event of a claim event. This is beneficial if you are seeking a hands-off approach, or as your portfolio grows.

Town planner

Town planners are responsible for the design and development of towns and cities, and understand the ins and outs of council regulations and policies. Having access to a knowledgeable town planner in the area where you've selected to purchase property is therefore invaluable for value-add projects such as developments, subdivisions or renovations. Without an experienced planner, specific conditions could be overlooked, which could stop a development project or magnify its costs if your application is rejected.

It's best to choose an independent town planner rather than the local council one. Independent town planners are generally more up to date, sprightly and willing to give information, as they'll hope that you will utilise their services at some stage.

Valuer

Property valuers estimate the value of your property by looking at comparable sales, estimating the land value, and looking at development potential and the demand for the type of property. It's their job to estimate the price you could realistically achieve for a property if it were given reasonable marketing. Experienced property valuers are a great source of information – they know their area well and will offer unbiased information.

CHAPTER TWENTY
SEARCHING FOR PROPERTIES

After researching and determining the general locations and types of properties you're interested in, you can start looking at properties in your price range. In a cold market, you can also look at properties at, say, $50,000 more than your price range, as you may be able to negotiate that down, or the price may drop if the property doesn't sell. However, in a hot market you will most likely have to do the opposite and set your search budget lower.

It's unlikely you'll find a property that you consider 100 per cent perfect; the aim is simply to find one that meets your criteria as closely as possible. Basically, there are two main ways to tackle your search: on-market sales and off-market sales.

On-market sales

'On market' properties are listed publicly and are available to view via the traditional pathway of advertising. There are three basic ways to find these properties:

1. real estate websites
2. real estate agents
3. buyer's agents.

If you establish good relationships with real estate agents in regions you favour, they'll contact you about potential properties. If you engage a buyer's agent, they will have existing relationships with selling agents.

When using real estate websites, you can speed up your search by applying filters for location, budget and type of property. The map view on these websites is a good way to choose a location, and also shows you how many similar properties are available in the area for sale. It's also worth checking Google's satellite images to look for potential greenfield developments in the area and comparing the Google Street View with the property advertisement photos.

As you probably already know, this aspect of property investing can be extremely time consuming. Not only do you have to consider the broader area – nearby amenities, parks, schools, shops, public transport and road access – but then you have to carry out due diligence on each potential property.

My tip is to make a short list, narrowing down to a few areas and to the specific types of property you're interested in. This will prevent you getting an overload of properties, and from there you can then choose a few to visit and make an offer on.

Here are some recommended resources for your property journey:

- **Realestate.com.au** and **Domain.com.au** are the largest property websites in Australia, where the majority of real estate for sale or rent across the country is available online. They allow you to keep up to date with what has recently sold in the areas you are tracking.

- **CoreLogic** is Australia's most comprehensive source of property data and analytics.

- **Walk Score** shows the walkability of a property or location and ranks the location compared to others in the suburb and state.

- **QuickStats** is a fast, simple way for users to understand an area at a glance. Provided by the ABS, it's intended for anyone who wants quick summary information about an area and can be very helpful when creating a short list of potential investment locations.

- **SQM Research** is a respected Australian investment research house headed by Louis Christopher. It specialises in providing ratings and data across all major asset classes.

- **.id** (which stands for 'informed decisions') provides a wealth of demographic data by suburb and demystifies the latest census data.

- **McCrindle Research**, run by demographer Mark McCrindle, provides some insightful infographics.

- **Microburbs** provides a collection of free reports including neighbourhood demographics, commute times, schools, crime rates, income levels and much more.

- **Suburb Trends** offers some excellent suburb maps and reports. Many are free, but other reports and data must be purchased.

- **The Reserve Bank of Australia** produces a chart pack of useful graphs and statistics.

It can be tricky to interpret all of the information that is freely accessible, as there is no 'right answer'. Therefore, the best resource is the collective opinions of a variety of experts and sales agents.

Off-market sales

'Off market' properties are sold without advertising; you won't see them on the real estate websites. Also, some properties have a 'pre-market' period, when real estate agents provide prospective buyers with a 'first look' before the properties go on market. So, how do you get to know about them?

A good way to find off-market properties is to develop good relationships with sales agents, perhaps after you've made an unsuccessful offer on a property. Another way is to engage a buyer's agent. I am biased, but I recommend buyer's agents because they will know of large numbers of 'secret' off-market properties that you wouldn't have access to, because they have fantastic databases and networks. These properties can be so highly sought after that there is no need to list them, with both parties knowing that they will sell very quickly. They are properties that may be more suitable for your needs, saving you time and money in the long run.

To find off-market properties and build relationships with agents, first build an email list of agents that sell the type of property you are looking for in the area where you want to buy. Then, send the same email every week to stay on their radar. In the email include:

- your name
- that you are finance-approved
- what you are looking for (e.g. a major renovation project)
- specifications (square metreage, number of bedrooms, etc.)
- suburbs (list a maximum of three)
- budget.

The process for negotiating an off-market sale will usually be the same as for a fixed-price listing, with communication via the sales agent or buyer's agent. Note that just because the property is off market doesn't mean it's better value; your due diligence process will remain the same.

Methods of sale

The method of sale dictates the way you put offers on properties, the terms of the contract, and the order in which due diligence and finance will occur prior to going under contract. The property's selling agent will inform potential buyers which method of sale is likely to be used. The most common methods used for residential purchasing are private sales and auctions.

Private sales

A private sale is when a property's potential buyers are invited to make offers to either the seller's agent or the seller directly. Sometimes called 'private treaty', it's one of the most common ways to sell a home in Australia and doesn't involve an auction.

Once a price is agreed, the buyer lodges a deposit and, in most cases, the process will enter a cooling-off period. You can still back out at this stage, but may have to forfeit some of your deposit, depending on which state or territory the purchase is being made in.

There are pros and cons of buying via private sale. Upsides include having the ability to negotiate price and terms and the time to do investigations; however, it's not a 100-per-cent transparent process, because you can't see the other bidders in the room.

Auctions

Auctions are generally held in a hot market or in very attractive locations; they're less common with cheaper properties. This high-risk method of buying should be left to knowledgeable investors.

You should complete the same level of due diligence before you make an offer at auction as with other methods of sale, including getting unconditional finance approval and paying for valuations. Also, ensure the building and pest inspections have been carried out prior to the auction day.

The auction process is one of the main methods agents choose because of its emotional value. Potential buyers can get too emotional during bidding and push the price up, which is exactly what the agents want. Know what you are prepared to pay and what price you would walk away at. Better still, ignore the reserve price, or even have someone bid on your behalf if you suspect you might not be able to hold back.

A 10 per cent deposit is due immediately after a successful auction. A smaller deposit can be negotiated before the auction, but this will usually incur legal costs that won't be recouped if you lose the auction. Lenders will usually give you the funds for a deposit at an auction if you're using other properties as security, but this can come at a higher interest rate during the settlement period.

If you don't or can't go through with the purchase after winning an auction, you will inevitably lose your deposit and potentially remain liable for any further losses and damages sustained by the seller – auctions are legally binding.

Types of listings

The two main types of listings are fixed-price listings and expressions of interest.

Fixed-price listings

The fixed-price sales process is the most common. Such listings may be indicated on websites by wording such as 'Price on application', 'Offers above $1.2 million' or 'Contact agent'.

It's wise to check whether properties advertised this way have previously failed to sell at auction or been advertised for a long time. You can check the sales and rental campaign history from sources such as CoreLogic.

Generally, a fixed-price listing produces a quick sale without the seller having to pay expensive auction costs or lose time on an expression of interest process. It also enables the seller to have the contract ready, subject to finance, which allows for many potential buyers. However, it can be a slow process if there are many buyers or the owner isn't desperate to sell. The ideal situation is a desperate seller who is more likely to accept a lower-than-market-price offer.

Fixed-price listings encourage open communication with the owner through the sales agent – you can work indirectly with them so that the sale benefits both parties. It means you can put forward your concerns to the seller to help with negotiating.

Expressions of interest

Expressions of interest (EOI) aren't binding, but you need to be aware that they can sometimes stipulate conditions that need to be adhered to should the actual contract be signed. This could include, for example, paying the seller's solicitor's fees. These are typically used when you have a more complicated deal, such as a development site, a full block of apartments, or rural property.

On an EOI, you specify your buying entity, your offer, the amount of deposit and the terms you would like in the contract, such as due diligence and settlement. Your conditions may entice a buyer – for instance, if you're paying cash. You don't have to have completed your due diligence when you submit an expression of interest, but you still need to allow time for it.

Some EOIs have closing dates and are used to gauge interest before an auction. Agents will often put pressure on you to come up with an offer, and might also play other buyers off against one another. EOIs can turn into silent auctions: interested parties are required to put their best offer in writing by a certain time and date, and the property is then sold to the highest bidder. Agents often refer to the 'auction before the auction' as a Dutch auction and use it if they receive multiple offers before the event.

An EOI evolves into a Dutch auction when a property is listed for private sale or auction and multiple buyers agree either to pay the advertised purchase price or a price that the vendor will accept. In a Dutch auction, the vendor has to agree to sell at the level of one of the offers and therefore has nothing to lose in seeking a higher price. It's advisable to stay away from Dutch auctions, as they're rarely advantageous to the buyer in terms of achieving a good purchase price.

The benefit of an EOI, however, is that you can negotiate seriously without having to spend money on legal fees, building and pest inspections, and valuations.

CHAPTER TWENTY-ONE
NEW VERSUS OLD

Buying new property versus old property is a talking point as old as time, and depending on who you ask, you'll get a different answer every time. However, there are a few cold hard facts behind the debate.

Buying 'old'

Over time, older properties are usually better than new. This is because new properties are often sold at a premium, whereas anything older tends to hold its value more. Compare it to buying a new car: as soon as you drive it out of the showroom, its value can drop by as much as 30 per cent. Also, because the value of land goes up and building value trends down – as the old saying goes, 'land appreciates, houses depreciate' – a greater proportion of the value of older properties is in the land rather than in the dwelling, and they'll achieve better capital growth than the market average.

An older property will have history and a proven resale value, which can offer peace of mind that the purchase is fair. You'll have access to the sales history over the years, where you'll be able to see that your investment will be sound and meet the needs of the market. Older properties are also generally more affordable than new properties, which means you may be at less risk of facing mortgage stress. When it comes to negotiating, you have the ability to negotiate for a fair price – vendors of old properties are often motivated to sell quickly, so you can use this to your advantage to negotiate a bargain.

Older properties are perfect for adding value, offering great potential through renovations and improvements. The renovations don't need to be significant, either – even a cosmetic makeover can improve value, rentability and return. Plus, the costs are tax-deductible.

Older properties are also usually in more established areas with strong lifestyle attractions, such as high-quality amenity and infrastructure. This translates to higher performance.

Cons

The big drawback is the unknown factor of maintenance. Things go wrong in older properties, so you'll need to be prepared and to have a cash buffer for when it happens – because it will, and often at unexpected times.

Older properties can also be less appealing for tenants to rent. Without the shiny new fittings, it can be a harder sell, and you can expect a lower return than from a new property. You also can't claim the same depreciation benefits that you get with new properties, following changes to tax legislation in 2017.

Case study

A unit built in 1974 in Burwood, Sydney, was purchased for $212,000 in 2005, and in 2016 was valued by the bank at $345,000 following a drop in the market. A sum of $20,000 was spent on renovation, including the kitchen and repainting.

This investment unit saw 53 per cent growth over 11 years (2005 to 2016) after adding the cost of renovations to the purchase price.

This property is positively geared: the rent pays for the interest on the loan and all of the expenses.

Buying 'new'

Buying new or off the plan offers excellent advantages over existing properties. The main benefit includes tax write-offs, which is where depreciation comes in: you can claim tax deductions for physical components of a new property, such as furnishing costs and materials. There are many deductions you can claim on a new property, so it's worth engaging a good property tax accountant who is aware of the various depreciation schedules. They tend to change a lot! For more information about available tax benefits, visit ato.gov.au.

For example, you can claim the cost of building the investment property as depreciation over 40 years, because this is the amount of time the ATO reports a building will last before it needs replacing. On a new building that cost $250,000 to build, your tax claim could be $6,250 (2.5 per cent per year). You may also be able to access government incentives such as the First Home Owners Grant. Plus, you only need to pay stamp duty on the land value when buying a house and land package (although you do pay 10 per cent GST on the build costs).

New properties are also attractive to buyers seeking a low-maintenance lifestyle. In turn, the better the amenities, the higher the rental price. The ability to attract good tenants means less vacancy, as your tenants will be happy to live there without wishing to move somewhere better. There are also fewer overheads, because almost everything is near new and under builder or appliance warranty, requiring minimal maintenance.

In addition, you'll be protected by Home Building Compensation (HBC) cover, formerly known as Home Warranty Insurance (HWI), which is a legal requirement in all states and territories except for Tasmania. It is also known as builders' warranty insurance (or 'the Home Building Compensation Fund' in NSW). Basically, builders of new properties must take out this insurance, which protects you in the event of a major building defect.

Cons

New properties are highly sought after by foreign buyers. This is because foreign buyers are only allowed to purchase new properties (according to the Foreign Investment Review Board's approval rules), which means often they're not the best value. This is exacerbated by the fact that the developer's margin and marketing costs are also factored into the price. Added to that, capital growth may be slower because you can't add value through renovations. Also, because land is usually limited when it comes to new property, there's less opportunity to add value through subdivision or adding property onto the block. Finally, new properties often have high strata fees associated with maintaining communal facilities such as gyms and pools, which could harm your cash flow.

For off-the-plan properties (properties bought before construction is completed), buyer beware. This strategy is highly speculative because you don't know what will be delivered; it is best left to investors with deep pockets. You will be asked to put down a deposit to secure the property, but as you won't be able to get a loan in advance, you may lose it if things change closer to settlement.

As a general market rule, newer properties tend to get first hit when the economy suffers a downturn. Older properties may hold their value a little better. This is because with new builds, the value of the asset is predominantly in the house, whereas older builds generally hold most of their value in the land.

Case study

A unit in Manly Vale, Sydney, was built in 2005, purchased for $315,000 and sold in 2016 for $425,000.

The property was newly built when it was purchased in 2005, so nothing was spent on renovations. However, there were building defects identified during construction, causing big problems with strata, including high strata fees.

The unit only grew 34.9 per cent over 11 years (2005 to 2016), despite Sydney prices doubling during this time period. This illustrates how units and apartments typically do not perform as strongly as properties with a land component.

High depreciation gave tax advantages; however, this increased the capital gains tax when selling.

The property was negatively geared, so the rent did not cover the interest on the loan and all of the expenses.

CHAPTER TWENTY-TWO
THE ACQUISITION PROCESS

Acquiring a property involves three main stages:

1. negotiations
2. the 'under contract' period
3. settlement.

1. Negotiations

Negotiations on a property can take hours or months, depending on the seller and how much back and forth there is. Both the price and the terms and conditions can be negotiated as part of the process. These negotiations are usually performed through the selling agent (unless it's a private sale negotiated directly with the owner) and can be formal or informal, verbal or written in the first instance.

It's worth pointing out that making an offer on a property is not a legal commitment (except at an auction) – it's only an indication to the agent that you're interested.

The art of property investing comes down to confidence. If you use the right negotiating style, selling agents will want to work with you because they believe they can secure a deal. Leave your ego at the door, and never believe that anyone is 'on your side'. After all, agents get paid to sell you the house for the absolute maximum they can get for it.

Let me reiterate here that before you start negotiations, it's important that you know the area well, are aware of comparable sales and rents, know how long the property has been on the market and have carried out your initial due diligence. All this information can be used to reduce the price. Know what the typical gross rental yields are before you negotiate, as well.

As I mentioned earlier, even though the agent represents the seller, she or he will want to work with you to secure the sale. The agent will highlight how good the tenant is, the growth potential of the property, other buyers' interest and that there are higher offers. You, by contrast, should focus on the negatives, using some of the details the tenant has given you or that you've uncovered from the research you've done. Also, try to understand what the selling agent's incentives may be – maybe they need a sale and might be willing to negotiate a little more than usual.

Check how long the property has been on market and whether it has failed at auction. If it has failed at auction, there may be some opportunity to make a lower offer. Try to find out why the owner is selling. Is it a rushed sale? Can you work with them to reduce the price? Note that although distressed sales do come up, they're rare, and often you'd be better off finding a solid deal elsewhere. You need to know the level of demand for the property you're interested in, too – high demand will limit your negotiation power, while low demand and high supply will increase it.

You're more likely to obtain a quick purchase if it's a cash or unconditional purchase and the sale is not subject to you obtaining finance. For this, it's important to know the demand for the type of property.

Your greatest strength in negotiation, however, is your ability to walk away from the deal. The agent will want to work with you and will chase you, and being overly keen can be detrimental to your position. Sometimes the agent may even tell you the lowest price the seller will accept, which will reveal how keen the seller is to sell and whether they have unrealistic expectations. Some agents will indicate very high prices to the seller to get them to sign with their agency and then, if the property is on the market for a month or two, bring down the seller's expectations at that point. It's quite reasonable for you to point out that the owner's expectations are too high. Ask questions too, and if you aren't happy with the responses, try and ask follow-up questions such as, 'Why do you say that?' Ask even if you know the answers – selling agents love to chat, and they may reveal something valuable about the sale.

The negotiation usually ends somewhere between the seller's expectation and the buyer's initial offer, so it's helpful to understand the seller's needs. They may not agree to a lower price but may consent to terms and conditions that suit you, such as a longer settlement. These are the usual negotiable terms when making an offer on a property:

- price
- settlement period
- agreement to undertake specific repairs or maintenance
- early access (usually for building maintenance or showing prospective tenants through)
- building and pest inspection periods
- finance periods
- building and pest inspection access
- deposit amount
- subject to development applications.

After you have exchanged contracts, the deposit is usually 5 to 10 per cent of the purchase price. You will get it back if you pull out of the contract over conditions such as building and pest inspections or finance. If you exit the contract not under a condition and it's during the cooling-off period, you may lose a small portion of the purchase price. Specific information for each state and territory is shown in Table 7. If you pull out after the cooling-off period, you can be liable for your full deposit as well as any damages caused to the seller.

Table 7: Cooling-off periods per state and territory

State/Territory	Length	Terms if exiting contract during cooling-off period
ACT	5 business days	Buyer forfeits 0.25% of purchase price to seller
NSW	5 business days (or 10 business days if bought off the plan)	Buyer forfeits 0.25% of purchase price to seller
NT	4 business days	Buyer can cancel the contract without explanation and without penalty
Qld	5 business days	Buyer forfeits 0.25% of purchase price to seller
SA	2 days	Buyer is entitled to full refund of any deposit paid of more than $100
Tas.	N/A	No cooling-off period mandated by law, so a cooling-off period will only apply if the buyer asks their lawyer to draft an extra clause into the contract and both parties accept
Vic.	3 business days	Buyer is entitled to a full refund of the deposit, less $100 or 0.2% of the purchase price (whichever is greater)

State/ Territory	Length	Terms if exiting contract during cooling-off period
WA	N/A	No cooling-off period mandated by law, so a cooling-off period will only apply if the buyer asks their lawyer to draft an extra clause into the contract and both parties accept

You should document all communication. Even if you have phone discussions with real estate agents, it's essential to have a soft copy of all communication as a backup and for record keeping. This applies even after you have bought a property. Agents love talking on the phone and not having a soft copy of records, as it means they can protect themselves from being liable for misinformation.

If any information is found to be incorrectly presented, this should be a reason for you to go back and negotiate the price, if applicable.

Tips for negotiations

The two rookie mistakes are to go low ball or offer too much. Going low ball is when you make an extremely low offer and then ultimately miss out because you refuse to budge. There's nothing inherently wrong with this, but you risk missing out on a suitable home for a price you would have been happy to pay. You will also lose agents' respect, and they will be less inclined to want to work with you on future properties because you won't be seen as a serious buyer. Offering too much, on the other hand, is great for the seller but not so much for you, and is best avoided.

If the agent asks you to make an offer, your offer should include:

- offer amount (the price you are willing to pay)
- deposit paid (how much cash you are putting down)

- subject to (conditions such as finance and building and pest inspections)
- settlement period (the time between the contract date and the completed transaction).

Get set, go!

There are three questions an agent could ask you to gauge how interested you are and much wiggle room you have in your offer – they are not trying to be nice to you! If you can have answers prepared for these three questions, you'll be well on your way to securing the property for a much better price:

1. If this offer is not accepted, just so I know, what would your next offer be?
2. If I list a property the same size but newer, would you be happy to pay more for it?
3. What it is that makes you want to live around here?

Now, it's your turn to arm yourself by asking the right questions:

- Why is the vendor selling?
- Is the vendor after a short or long settlement period?
- Did the vendor do any work to the home before putting it on the market?
- How long has the vendor owned the property?
- Has the property been an investment or owner-occupied?
- How long has it been on the market?
- What's the lowest price the vendor will accept?
- Apart from the listing price, what would the perfect offer look like to the vendor?

Here's an example of an opening gambit in a negotiation:

'I'm doing my research on local three-bedroom houses and like the look of 15 Smith St. My budget is up to $1 million; am I wasting my time on this one?'

(Price range of comparable properties is between $900,000 and $1.1 million.)

Based on your research, you're offering the middle ground at $1 million. You want to know if your ballpark price is competitive or if it's too low, with buyer interest exceeding this already.

More often than not, the selling agent will say, 'Yes, definitely come and see it', or, 'No, don't bother – we have interest above that range already'.

By framing your question this way, you'll know over the phone whether or not you're wasting your time.

Both the seller and buyer need to feel they have negotiated a good deal, so try to reach a win-win solution, and follow up your verbal offer on a property with an email to the agent. As I said before, leave your ego behind and never become emotionally involved or committed to making the purchase. Don't get defensive if the negotiation doesn't go your way, either. Looking at multiple properties at the same time, rather than focusing on one property, will make this easier. Mentioning other properties that you're looking at can encourage the selling agent to try to secure a deal, too.

If you walk away from a purchase, tell the agent why and what price would attract you, as the property may stay on the market and the agent may come back to you later. Also ask the agent to keep an eye out for similar properties – this encourages them to work with you on the current deal as well as future deals.

Showing common courtesy to the selling agent if your offer isn't accepted is crucial. Being polite doesn't show weakness – rather, it shows that you're confident, understand the process and aren't emotionally invested. This may encourage the selling agent to work with you in the future and even send you properties prior to them hitting the market.

Other tips and tricks include the following:

- Look at comparable sales in the area so you know what the property is worth.

- Calling agents has a higher impact than emailing. Agents live on their phones!

- Understand the seller's objectives and try to be as accommodating as possible to beat other offers. For example, if the owners or tenants don't know where they will move, you could offer a lease-back period in your contract.

- Be prepared to negotiate the settlements or clauses.

- Know your property price limit and be prepared to walk away.

- Remember that the vendor is a living, breathing and probably lovely person – treating them as such will give you a much better chance of securing the property.

2. The 'under contract' period

Before you sign the contract, your conveyancer or solicitor will review it to ensure no major or initial red flags arise; they will usually examine it more closely once your offer is verbally accepted. Once the contract is exchanged and signed, you will need to engage and liaise with your conveyancer or solicitor; organise a building and pest inspection, strata inspection or any required pre-purchase reports; organise finance; and perform due diligence.

Building and pest reports, strata reports, valuations and searches cost money, so try to minimise the legal, finance and due diligence costs by first doing the items that are free, such as area and tenant research. Never stay in a deal just because you've invested some funds, though – the due diligence costs are minimal compared with the financial hit you'll take by purchasing an unsuitable property.

Once you have completed a building and pest inspection, it is vital to review this as soon as possible. Any items picked up in the report can either kill the deal or be a great negotiating tool to achieve a price reduction.

3. Settlement

Before you settle on a property, it's essential that you're satisfied with it and you're prepared for settlement day. Your solicitor will ensure most of the legal and registration matters are taken care of, but you need to arrange the following:

- **Organising insurance:** If something happens to the property between exchange of contracts and settlement, having adequate insurance will give you peace of mind. In many states in Australia, the risk of the property passes to the buyer after settlement; in some, it's at the time of exchange.

- **Collecting keys, passes and codes:** Make sure you know who has the keys and when you can collect them from the agent or your conveyancer or solicitor. Also, make sure you have the alarm codes (if any) and instruction manuals. Most agents will have the keys to hand over; however, if there is no agent, you might collect them from your conveyancer or solicitor. By sorting out the logistics beforehand, you can ensure there are no delays or problems later.

- **Pre-settlement inspection:** This is to ensure the property is in the same condition as when you performed your earlier inspections. For vacant properties, this is critical to ensure no damage has occurred or rubbish been left behind. Even if the property is tenanted and the tenant is responsible for the property, an inspection is still recommended, though it's not as essential. Normally, your property manager will arrange it free of charge, as they will use the meeting to introduce themselves to the tenant and get a condition report.

- **Shortfall money for settlement:** Your conveyancer or solicitor will provide you with a breakdown of funds, usually a week or a few days prior to settlement. However, it's best to start transferring money to where it needs to go early on to prevent last-minute issues. If funds that are to be borrowed are coming from a lender, the lender must have the authorisation present to draw on these funds. The conveyancer or solicitor will also calculate the adjustments required for rates and other council fees. Note that the seller is responsible for these up to and including the day of settlement, and these costs are usually calculated pro rata to the date of settlement. Make sure that the cheques have the correct spellings to avoid delays.

Foreign investment

Australia has compelling investment qualities compared with other countries around the world and therefore attracts a lot of interest from those seeking to capitalise on our capital growth opportunities. In fact, combined investment in commercial and residential real estate from foreign buyers totalled $87.8 billion in the 2020–21 financial year, according to the Foreign Investment Review Board's (FIRB) annual report, outstripping investment in all other industries.

Foreign investment comes with a number of rules and its own application process, as imposed by the FIRB, from whom investors need to seek permission before buying property here. This is because foreign investments are deemed high risk. The restrictions include the following:

- Foreign investors can only buy new dwellings, not established, as part of a view that buying new offers more growth opportunities for the country as a whole. The overarching policy is that the investment should increase housing supply. The dwelling must not have been occupied for more than 12 months.

- Foreign investors can buy vacant land, but a property must be constructed within four years of FIRB approval.
- They can be granted approval to redevelop an existing property, because this is in line with job and economy growth.
- Only temporary Australian residents can purchase an established dwelling, and must sell it when eventually leaving the country.
- Typically, they have to front up with a larger deposit than the typical 20 per cent.

How much does the FIRB process typically cost?

The FIRB process fee is dependent upon the value of the property, as shown in Table 8.

Table 8: FIRB process fees

Value	Fee
Less than $75,000	$2,000
$1 million or less	$6,350
>$1 million to $2 million	$12,700
>$2 million to $3 million	$25,400
>$3 million to $4 million	$38,100
>$4 million to $5 million	$50,800
>$5 million to $6 million	$63,500
>$6 million to $7 million	$76,200
>$7 million but less than $8 million	$88,900
>$8 million but less than $9 million	$101,600
>$9 million but less than $10 million	$114,300

How does the FIRB process work?

If you're a foreign investor, it's always best to seek legal advice before going down this path, as you'll need to ensure you comply with all of the FIRB's requirements. Generally, it takes 30 days for them to make a decision on your application.

If you are an Australian citizen living overseas – or have dual citizenship – and want to buy a property back home, the strict foreign investment laws don't affect you. However, securing finance is typically more difficult if you are overseas earning a foreign currency, even if you are an Australian citizen: banks will usually only take a percentage of your income (or may reject you entirely, depending on the currency), and if they give you a loan it will have a higher deposit and interest-rate requirement. Again, a mortgage broker will be able to assist you to navigate financing a purchase from your position overseas.

CHAPTER TWENTY-THREE
SELLING PROPERTIES

Selling a property is a tough decision. Ideally, you want to hold on to your properties long term, as they're delivering you an income. So, before you consider selling, run the numbers carefully and calculate your return on the property, taking into account the stamp duty, purchasing costs, selling costs and capital gains tax. Remember, if you're planning to sell the property and replace it with another, you'll need to pay stamp duty and purchasing costs again – and this can add up to more than 10 per cent of the cost of the property, just to swap one property for another.

There are a few reasons why investors don't sell their properties. First, property is a top-performing asset class – over the long term, the median house price continues to trend upwards. You can also leverage one property to buy another, and your tenants are effectively paying your mortgages indefinitely. Also, if you sell, you pay tax on 50 per cent of the property's capital gains (its increase in value); instead, you could refinance the equity into another property, or redraw equity.

You might choose to sell:

- when it's a seller's market – that is, there are lots of buyers in the market and you can achieve a top price

- if the market looks to be heading into a downturn – it may be worth selling before the herd is aware (remember the market phases we looked at in chapter 18)
- when interest rates are rising and you believe the market might go flat or turn
- if you believe that rents won't increase in the near to medium future and there are better opportunities available to you
- when selling is part of an exit strategy (we'll look at this in more detail later in this chapter)
- if part of your portfolio review process reveals a property that is underperforming and, based on your research and assumptions, will continue to underperform in the future.

Obviously, you might also choose to sell if you get a great offer for the property – say, for example, if a developer offers an above-market price. Generally, the long-term history of property shows that selling is a bad idea unless you are moving that money to a higher-quality asset or better opportunity.

You shouldn't sell if:

- it's a buyer's market
- the area the property is in is gentrifying and has growth prospects
- interest rates are dropping
- the market is still growing.

Don't sell a property just because you don't 'like' it, either – property investing is about the numbers! I find that so many people sell properties because they continually have minor maintenance issues. The few thousand dollars a year they pay seems like a huge headache, but if the property is growing tens of thousands per year it is still a great investment!

Let's say, however, that you're considering selling because the value of the property has grown significantly and you need funds to invest in a better project. Ask yourself:

- How does selling fit into my plan?
- Where will I put the profits?
- How leveraged is my portfolio?
- What's my risk profile?
- What's my exit strategy?

Preparation for selling

If you do decide that selling is a wise idea, there are a few steps that will help you achieve the best price. If you have a tenant, increase the rents to market value if you haven't already done so. If it's an investor market, try to get tenants on leases that are as long as possible. Also, make cosmetic improvements to the property – for example, fresh paint, upgraded flooring or a revamp of the landscaping (if there are garden or lawn areas) might help present the property in its best light.

House staging

House staging (or 'styling') is where you pay a company to bring in their own décor during the sales campaign. They will expertly arrange their furniture and dress up your home in the hopes that buyers will pay more for it.

Staging has been shown to boost your home's perceived value, appealing to emotional buyers. It can also mean a faster selling time, because it sparks interest quickly in potential buyers.

You can expect to spend about $5,000 on home staging, which covers not only the professional photo shoot but the duration of your campaign.

Exit strategies

When you're investing in property of any kind, you need to have an exit strategy before you begin; choosing one should be part of your preparatory planning. Each investor's exit strategy will be different, depending on their goals, their portfolio and personal circumstances – a financial planner may be helpful here to provide advice on what could be most appropriate for you. Your strategy may change as your circumstances alter, but it can guide the decisions you make along the way.

Some investors will transition over time to higher-cash-flow properties, such as commercial property, to build a larger passive income. If you are interested in commercial property, please refer to my other book: *Commercial Property Investing Explained Simply*.

Here are six of the most common exit strategies you could use when looking to capitalise on your residential investments:

1. keeping all your properties and not paying down your debt
2. keeping all your properties but paying down your debt
3. keeping all your properties and increasing your debt
4. selling part of your portfolio to pay down your debt
5. selling part of your portfolio and living off the profit
6. selling your whole portfolio.

1. Keeping all your properties and not paying down your debt

Keeping all your properties and not paying down your debt is the fastest way to build a passive income, but it carries a lot of risk.

With this strategy, generating a passive income from accumulation is the key focus, rather than from paying down the debt. Once you have an adequate portfolio and your desired cash flow, you stop buying more properties, and even though you maintain the same level of debt, over time the properties will probably increase in value. As rents increase but the mortgage amount stays the same, your passive income will increase.

The risk with this strategy is that you can be exposed to property price swings and prolonged increases in interest rates, and you can also be more greatly affected financially if the properties become vacant.

Some people may decide to pay down their debt slowly using any surplus cash flow, but with this strategy it's not the main focus: the principal objective is to generate a passive income to provide financial freedom.

2. Keeping all your properties but paying down your debt

If you keep all your properties but pay down your debt, you stop buying properties before retirement so that you leave enough time for the cash flow from the properties – and your own savings from your employment – to accumulate enough to pay off the debt. You can achieve the same cash flow as the first strategy with a smaller portfolio size, because once the loan is paid off you don't have the interest expense to pay. Also, once you own the portfolio outright, a lot of the risk is mitigated as there's no debt. This makes it easier to manage even vacant properties.

However, this is a long strategy. Not everyone starts their property journey early enough to be able to pay down all their debt before retirement. Also, it's not easy to pay down debt quickly if you have a large portfolio!

3. Keeping all your properties and increasing your debt

The third strategy involves continually refinancing your properties to live on the extracted equity. Instead of living off a purely passive income (generated only from cash flow), you're also living off capital growth – as your properties go up in value over time, you can draw portions of that increased equity to live on. However, to maintain the same passive income, you'll need your rents to go up enough to counteract the increased mortgage repayments required due to the equity withdrawal. With this strategy, you need a larger portfolio to generate enough cash flow to keep servicing your loans.

Living off capital growth has been made difficult due to the recent Australian Prudential Regulation Authority (APRA) crackdown on responsible lending. This strategy may have worked in the past but doesn't really work in the current lending environment.

This is the highest-risk strategy as it's the most susceptible to market cycles, vacancy levels and lending fluctuations.

4. Selling part of your portfolio to pay down your debt

The most common exit strategy is to sell part of your portfolio and use the proceeds to pay down the debt on your remaining properties when you retire from formal employment. Obviously, you need to have multiple properties to employ this strategy. Usually, the plan is to sell lower-yielding properties to pay off the higher-yielding ones and maximise the cash flow for your retirement.

Most investors will stagger the selling of the properties over several years in order to minimise capital gains tax liabilities by keeping themselves in a lower tax bracket.

5. Selling part of your portfolio and living off the profit

The strategy of selling your properties in stages and living off the proceeds from each sale is typically used by investors who need a higher income. The downside is that every time you sell a property, you reduce your passive income and miss out on future capital growth.

6. Selling your whole portfolio

Selling your whole portfolio is usually part of a conservative strategy in which the funds are placed in a low-risk savings account to provide an income during retirement. Some people may diversify their profits into other investments to mitigate risk. This is quite a rare strategy, as property is generally seen as a stable investment, depending on the type and location.

Investors will sometimes choose this strategy if they have enough superannuation to live on and want to give the proceeds from property sales to family members.

CHAPTER TWENTY-FOUR
PROPERTY MANAGEMENT

Managing a tenanted residential property may seem easy at first glance, but there's quite a lot more to it than simply collecting the rent. Therefore, many investors choose to outsource the day-to-day running of an investment property to a professional property manager.

The right property manager can be the difference between a property that is tenanted long term and a vacant one. Your relationship with the manager is a partnership. You're looking for a long-term relationship, as the manager will be instrumental in ensuring that your property produces a positive result. You need good rapport and communication so that the manager understands your objectives and finds the right tenants for your space. When you leverage other people's time and expertise, the percentage of gross rental income you pay is money well spent. The larger the number of properties you own, the more time you would need to spend self-managing them – be careful!

Look for a property manager who sees their job as about relationship-building, not just completing transactions. Their focus should be on increasing the value of your asset while maintaining and increasing cash flow each year.

Using a property manager

At the most basic level, your property management agency's responsibility is to prioritise your best interests when making decisions for your house or apartment.

The right property manager can make all the difference to your investment. They will save you time and money over the long term and help make key decisions around the property, so it's worth engaging someone who can become intrinsic to growing your portfolio.

Here are some of the tasks a property manager undertakes:

- setting rents – property managers have in-depth market knowledge and understand the maximum tenants are willing to pay
- collecting arrears (or delayed income)
- interviewing tenants (checking their history with previous landlords, their rental history and if they paid on time, what professions they have, their profile, and so on)
- maintenance – property managers ensure the property is in good condition for the tenants, and good property managers use their network of trusted technicians and tradies to ensure you're getting the best quotes
- routine inspections
- all property-related payments, including settling utility and water bills, council rates and strata levies
- documenting all the information relevant to your rental property for you
- maintaining efficient communication and being responsive to both tenants' and owners' requests
- representing you at tribunal if there are disputes with your tenants that cannot be resolved with non-legal mediation – they'll support your case with evidence, such as records of late

payments, photographs of any damages to property, receipts, and copies of letters and any other correspondence

- understanding and keeping up with current laws and regulations related to rental property – in the case that either party oversteps the legal boundaries expected from a landlord–tenant relationship, it is much easier for your property manager to navigate this than if you self-manage because they must stay on top of any new legislation (such as new fire alarm legislation, for example).

Adequately maintaining the property is one of the most important aspects of effective property management. Not only is this a requirement for landlord insurance, it is also crucial in cases of nightmare tenants. Having confidence in someone who can chase up rent arrears and manage property damage or illegal activities professionally and with as little stress as possible is just as important as them having the skills, experience and resources to identify and place good tenants in the first place.

Finding a manager who has experience in your property's type (such as apartment, townhouse or stand-alone house) will give you a better outcome. Local knowledge is extremely important, and obviously you need them to be close by to handle tenant issues. You also want your manager to have a good reputation in the community.

The manager also, of course, needs to be up to date with modern digital resources and must digitise all hard-copy media, such as bills, maintenance invoices and cheques received.

One point to be aware of is that the selling agent for a property you've purchased may push to manage it themselves after the sale. However, just because they sold the property doesn't necessarily mean they're the best person to manage it. One of the best ways to find a good manager is through referral from another property investor – there are now many residential property investor groups online, so asking for referrals has become relatively easy.

Remember to check online reviews, too, to see how they have been rated by others.

Here are some questions you should ask prospective property management businesses:

- How long has your dedicated property manager been at the business, and what's their previous management experience?
- How many properties does the business manage?
- How many properties does your dedicated property manager manage? (Typically any more than 150 and their service may drop in quality.)
- Does your dedicated property manager have a personal assistant?
- How often are routine inspections carried out?
- Could you give me some examples of other properties you manage in the area?
- What's the typical time to re-let a property similar to mine? Could you give me some examples?
- How do you run your marketing campaigns?
- What's the procedure for tenant reviews?
- What's the procedure for collecting arrears?
- Do you offer private inspections?
- What days and times are your property managers available for inspections?
- Who will be managing my property?
- Do you outsource entry, routine or exit inspections?
- Can you handle bills such as rates and water?
- What is your portfolio's average vacancy rate – that is, what percentage of the properties you manage are vacant at any one time?
- How do you screen prospective tenants?

Self-management versus using a property manager

If you want to manage your property yourself, you'll save on the commission that the manager would earn. This usually ranges from 6 to 12 per cent of the weekly rent (depending on the price of rent and the quality of the service), in addition to other fees such as letting, marketing, lease renewal and representation at tribunals.

This arrangement can become problematic if you are friendly with the tenants, or if they know that the property is self-managed. They may take advantage of your position as the property manager, especially when it comes to enforcing the lease agreement.

You need to be fully aware of the applicable rental laws and understand your obligations. As far as the law is concerned, ignorance is no defence. Many states and territories have recently amended (or are implementing changes to) tenancy legislation to reflect this.

If your property manager fails to deliver the advantages you expect from them or doesn't run things properly, this will translate to a poor ROI. However, the same outcome could occur if you don't have the time to self-manage your property properly.

Self-managing also means that being a borderless investor is near impossible – you will need to buy in your local area.

Engaging a property manager

Once you have chosen a property manager, they will send you the paperwork needed to authorise them to carry out management activities. Many property managers will let you sign the documents electronically, usually through DocuSign.

After this, if you previously managed the property yourself or you're moving from another management service, you'll need to provide the following to your new manager:

- the lease agreements
- copies of current and outstanding invoices

- the dates on which each tenant pays rent
- how much any bonds are for and where they're held
- whether outgoings are paid on demand or allocated monthly, and the current amount.

The manager will then contact each of your tenants about future procedures.

If you've just purchased the property, you'll need to provide your new manager with the settlement statement.

Ideally, at this point, your work is largely finished and you'll have a 'set and forget' property.

How much is property management?

Unfortunately, it's not as simple as a single number or percentage. Property management fees are generally divided into a few categories:

- ongoing management fee
- property management leasing fee
- a range of miscellaneous fees and charges.

It's important when comparing property management fees that you understand exactly what you are getting in each fee proposal, even if a proposal claims to be all-inclusive. Each property manager will charge different amounts, and you may not be comparing apples with apples.

Your property manager should give you a list of all the associated fees before you sign a contract, so everything is broken down. Don't forget that GST is payable on these fees, too, so ensure you're clear on whether the price includes it or it's additional.

Typical fee structure

All fees can be negotiated. For instance, you could handle a rent review yourself and perhaps save yourself a small fee. Be aware, however, that cutting the agent out of earning income will not get them in your corner and looking out for your best interests. It's best to negotiate any such reductions before you engage the manager, and to record the details of the agency agreement. Beware of hidden fees – some managers will charge you for each extra service.

You also may need to pay additional fees for tasks such as:

- letting and lease renewal (based on around one or two weeks of the property's rent; lease renewal negotiation is sometimes included in this fee but can also be a separate fee of $25 to $100)
- administration (around $5 to $10 per month)
- signage and advertising (usually ranges from $100 to $500)
- tenancy database checks (about $12 per person)
- file preparation and tribunal attendances (usually ranges from $100 to $200 following disputes between tenants and landlords)
- preparation of the end of financial year statement ($25 to $50)
- making insurance claims (a fee might be payable if you have a landlord insurance policy and your tenants left without paying the last month's rent – expect up to $150).

Which structure is better: separate or all-inclusive?

The most common approach for investors and owners is to pay it all separately – where the property management fee is charged separately from the letting fee and ancillary costs – instead of all-inclusively. However, it comes down to individual needs. Some prefer an all-inclusive fee because they can budget more accurately, while others like to keep things separate. Generally, when companies bundle fees together, they work it out on the basis that you'll need a new tenant about every twelve months; if you have higher turnover than that, you'll save money, but if you have the same tenant for two or three years then you'll end up paying more. It's worth noting that a lower percentage fee is not necessarily cheaper, nor is a more expensive agency necessarily better.

Table 9 illustrates a typical fee structure, which shows the possible fees during the property ownership.

Table 9: A typical property management fee structure

Fee	Property Manager 1	Property Manager 2
Management (when rent is $700 per week)	6.5% + GST = $2,366 + GST	7.5% + GST = $2,730 + GST
Signage	$120	included
Photography	$350	included
Inspection fee	$185	included
Leasing preparation	$33	included
Initial leasing	$700	$700
Leasing renewal	$225	included
End-of-year statements	$0	included
Monthly admin	$5.50 ($66 per annum)	included
Total per annum	**$4,045 + GST**	**$3,430 + GST**

PART V
DUE DILIGENCE

As I've mentioned before, due diligence is the most important part of buying a property. It's a lot of work, but it's essential to determine whether a property is a quality asset. The purpose of due diligence is to discover current or potential problems with a property, understand its upside and verify the information obtained. This will help you negotiate the correct price for the property.

A checklist to help you conduct due diligence is available for download at www.paliseproperty.com.

CHAPTER TWENTY-FIVE
INITIAL DUE DILIGENCE

Some investors perform only cursory due diligence and accept the data provided by the agent as gospel. It's crucial not to assume anything, though: all facts and figures need to be cross-checked. Undertaking thorough due diligence can reduce the stress of a purchase, give you more confidence and ensure your negotiation skills are first-class. Your analysis needs to be at least as good as – if not better than – the lender's valuation.

Having said that, it's easy to get analysis paralysis with due diligence, so take a high-level view first. Many investors become too focused on insignificant issues that stop them making a quality purchase, and complicate and lengthen the buying decision. No property is perfect: just run as many numbers as possible to determine whether it's a sound investment. The fundamentals of due diligence are the same whether you're buying a property worth $300,000 or $30 million.

When you're starting out, it's best to become an expert in one particular property type, as each type has its own idiosyncrasies; understanding the differences will increase the chances of your success.

Initial information

The first step in due diligence is to gather critical information so that you can decide whether to shortlist the property and investigate further. If the preliminary checks are positive, you can progress to more detailed due diligence. As discussed in chapter 22, you may be able to leave it until you have the property under contract if the contract is subject to inspection and due diligence clauses; however, detailed due diligence must be performed beforehand if you're proposing to buy at auction or are taking a contract without conditions.

Here are some questions to ask the sales agent to assist your initial inquiries. Don't ask them all at once, though, or during your first conversation with the agent, as you might disgruntle them from the start!

- How long has the property been on the market?
- How many offers have you had already?
- Why is the owner selling?
- Is the owner interested in a short or long settlement?
- Will you be listing similar properties soon?
- Could you please provide some comparable sales?
- Is the tenant up to date with rent and outgoings?
- Has the owner ever needed to offer rent abatements (discounts)?
- What's the land tax value on the property?
- When does the current tenant's lease expire (if there is one)?
- Is the tenant currently paying market rent?
- How long has the current tenant been at the property?

CHAPTER TWENTY-SIX
AREA AND PROPERTY RESEARCH

Understanding the region you're buying in is a crucial part of your detailed due diligence. The region will affect how your property performs in the short and long term in terms of tenant success, vacancy rates and capital growth – all key factors that require careful consideration.

Understanding the macro- and micro-economics of the area will tell you the long-term growth patterns, and which areas are likely to be up and coming with high population growth.

It's not unusual for investors to fear buying in an area they're not familiar with, but with modern technology everything can be researched remotely, so there's no reason not to look in other locations, even interstate.

Area types

Let's look at a few typical areas in which to buy.

Inner city

Properties in the inner city come with many benefits. They generally mean a shorter commute to work, and they also enjoy close proximity to shopping, entertainment and recreational activities. Some residents may feel more connected and live a more vibrant lifestyle. For investors, higher interest in the area can mean higher-income tenants, and this can make it easier to sell properties quicker (such as at auction or off market).

However, they can also come with drawbacks. For a start, you're generally looking at apartments, because houses in inner-city areas are often unaffordable for the general population. There can be an oversupply in apartments, which may lead to slower capital growth or lower rental income, and some lenders may only lend up to 70 per cent if the apartment building is high density (they make their decision based on many factors, such as the complex, the suburb and supply in the area). Also, many apartment blocks are poor-quality structures with high maintenance costs for the owners' corporation, and thus high strata costs.

Blue-chip areas

Blue-chip areas are desirable urban areas, such as those near coast-lines, in the middle ring of a city, near cafe hubs or around natural reserves. They tend to attract a higher-income demographic and a large percentage of PPOR (principal place of residence) ownership. The high demand means generally stable market fluctuations and little supply on the market (because most PPOR residents don't intend to sell, creating even more scarcity), as well as historically higher capital growth. Also, if you own a property in a blue-chip area, you can claim most losses, including depreciation.

The main drawback is that properties in these areas are harder to acquire, because it's difficult for most people to afford 20 per cent deposits on multi-million-dollar properties. This often means they have to be negatively geared and have low cash flow (so the repairs and expenses have to be covered partly by you). Your borrowing capacity may also be hurt by the negative gearing.

Regional areas

The ABS predicts that Australia's population will double by 2075. Some regional areas are likely to experience a significant increase in population and, in turn, demand. Regional areas can be attractive to investors because house prices are much more affordable, and properties have higher cash flow from the start – for example, Cairns, Townsville and the Hunter region have high rental yields. They are often close to nature and have open spaces, walking and cycling trails, reserves and beaches nearby. There is generally potential to add value through repairs and renovations, as well as potential for gentrification, as the increasingly popular work-from-home lifestyle allows more tenants and PPOR owners to live outside the CBD. Infrastructure and developments happening in regional areas also give the population room to grow.

The main drawback is that the future cannot be predicted with certainty. Generally, regional areas will have a less diverse range of industry and employment, which means they are more susceptible to the impact of one of these industries declining. Also, some regional areas have higher unemployment, lower income and higher crime rates, and destruction of property and other tenant complications are more common. The potential for growth can offset these factors, but population growth may not be enough to sustain capital growth, and the town may not gentrify. It can also be harder to sell as there's potentially high supply, greenfield areas and generally not an abundance of buyers like in capital cities (it's rare to see auctions in regional areas as there is not enough demand and competition); this can water down any gains.

Specialised regions

Sometimes specialised regions can have their own unique circumstances. The mining towns in the north of Western Australia are an example of this. During the mining boom, when the construction of massive mining projects fuelled an unsustainable economic boom, population and demand for properties increased dramatically, as workers needed somewhere to stay. Investors saw the high yields and property prices soared due to new demand.

However, the mining demand slowed, and the mining industry shed 46,000 full-time jobs between 2013 and 2015. There was no longer enough demand or population to absorb the inflated rental or property prices. Property prices were more than halved, and rental yields were cut by 80 to 90 per cent. Median house prices in Newman (1,186 kilometres northeast of Perth), for example, dropped from $850,000 in 2012 to $153,000 in 2016. Investors were left unable to pay their mortgages due to a lack of rental income and unable to sell for an amount that would pay their debts.

This example highlights the dangers of relying on a single-sector economy and, hence, the importance of a diverse, resilient and strong economy representing multiple growth drivers.

Gentrifying areas

The value of property and the market perception of an area can change due to gentrification, and you need to be aware of this when it comes to where you invest. Basically, gentrification is the change in fortune of a particular area. This is typically the result of middle- and upper-class individuals moving into the area and investing their time, money and resources. In turn, this starts to affect other elements in the area, such as amenities, infrastructure and employment opportunities, and can ultimately lead to an increase in property prices.

There are six stages of gentrification, and by understanding these you can time your entry to pick the next 'hotspot' and best new markets to invest in:

1. **Discussions:** These usually take place in council or chamber of commerce meetings about what changes will be taking place and when.

2. **Planning:** Plans of the changes are drawn and written up.

3. **New innovations:** New places such as hospitals, schools and shops are great for gentrifying an area.

4. **Intensive development:** Development brings new employment sectors and pioneering projects, which bring in talent.

5. **Population movement:** Socio-economic change starts to occur, with the number of wealthier people in the area increasing.

6. **Gentrification takes off:** Property values rise.

Borderless investing

Borderless investing means investing in property that is in another state or region to where you live. It is important to diversify risk. Borderless investing can help with this, as each property market – Adelaide, Brisbane, Sydney, and so on – moves at different speeds and in different cycles.

This means that for most Australians, the best-performing growth market at any given time won't be the same area they are living in. People have a tendency to favour areas they are familiar with. When they 'research' their area, it's common to only look for facts that support their ready-made, preconceived opinion. 'If I like the suburb, others will too' is a big misconception. It's important to remain objective and look more broadly.

Another reason to pursue borderless investing is that if all your properties are in the same state or territory, you may pay a higher land tax fee, as some states and territories have higher land tax rates than others (see chapter 14).

Area research

Once you've homed in on an area type, there are several metrics to investigate to determine what specific areas you should target. Let's take a look at some of these metrics in more detail.

Comparable sales and rentals in the area

You need to know what similar properties have sold for in the same market. This will give you a good foundation upon which to set your price expectations. Go to as many open homes and auctions as possible, so that you really begin to understand the market.

Take into account building materials, block size, era, slope of the land, aspect, views, number of bathrooms and bedrooms (be honest about whether that fourth bedroom is actually an office), renovations that have occurred, and the quality of the finishes and other aspects. If the house next door is identical and on an identical block, and it sold for $650,000 yesterday, you would likely be correct to expect the same result for your property; however, if your block is smaller, or if your house has been renovated less recently, you'd be right to potentially revise your expectations downwards.

Median house price

The median house price is essentially the sale price of the home in the middle of a list of sales, where the sales are arranged in order from lowest to highest price. Understanding the median price is helpful when looking at comparable sales.

Median house prices are better looked at with a long-term view. A 10 per cent increase in the suburb's median house price doesn't necessarily suggest that house prices in the area will rise across the board. If a number of multi-million-dollar homes came onto the market and all sold last month, this would raise the median price, but the value of your more moderately priced home may not have changed at all.

The median house price is only useful to know if you are looking at similar properties – that is, middle-of-the-range properties. If you are looking in a beachside suburb, for instance, a property two streets back from the beach will have a completely different price to a property 10 streets back. The median price is also more useful the more sales that have occurred in the area; for example, if there have only been two applicable sales in the location you are assessing, the data pool is too small to produce meaningful results.

Another factor to consider is that there can be a lag in the reported data you see from certain sources. For example, some prices reported may have been negotiated as much as six months prior, with settlement 45 to 60 days after that. Simply relying on suburb reports that are six months behind can put you out of touch with the market. This is where using a buyer's agent can become invaluable. They have a strong handle on the market and are on the ground speaking and transacting with agents in that market daily.

Auction clearance rate

The auction clearance rate is the percentage of auctions that result in a successful sale – either at auction, before auction or just after auction. This varies across different markets, but the trend is an excellent indication of the current level of demand. For example, during COVID-19 lockdowns, the clearance rate was historically low because auctions weren't able to be held. After this period, clearance rates skyrocketed due to the build-up of buyers.

Days on market

'Days on market' indicates the average number of days it takes to sell a property in that location. This is an excellent indication of the level of demand in a particular suburb. Obviously, the fewer days properties spend on market, the more demand exists in that suburb.

Vacancy rates

Vacancy rates indicate the proportion of vacant rental property in relation to all available properties in an area. It is calculated as a percentage of dwellings in an area that are unoccupied within a particular time period. You can use the vacancy rate to project a fairly accurate ROI for a rental property and how secure its rental income is.

You don't want your property to remain empty for weeks or months (or even longer) before it is rented. If your property is vacant, you're losing good rental income, which can start impacting on your other investments. A vacancy rate of 3 per cent is considered healthy because it represents a market balanced between tenants and owners. Note that you may deliberately choose an area with a higher vacancy rate than this in order to purchase at a lower price, or because the area offers higher rental yields; however, higher vacancy rates do not necessarily correlate with higher rental yields, and the benefits of a lower purchase price may be offset by a lower ROI due to the higher vacancy rate.

Buying the right house in the right area will help reduce vacancy rates from the start, but there are a few other options, too:

- Ensure your lease agreements expire during a good period for renting. Typically, January and February or June and August are when a lot of renters are looking.

- Appeal to your market. For example, properties in hotter regions will require air conditioning, and properties in areas with lots of families will be more attractive if they have large backyards.

- Reduce the rent. A $30 rent reduction on your $750-per-week property may seem steep at first, but if it can reduce your vacancy period by more than two weeks, you're still ahead in the end. Always think of the long game.

- Let your agent know you're willing to do work to the property if requested by prospective tenants: for example, replacing dated appliances, re-carpeting rooms that are looking old and worn, or replacing flyscreens that are wearing through.

- Use good photography to advertise your property.

- Look after your current tenants and attend to any maintenance items as they arise.

Body corporate review

When land is subdivided and registered under the *Land Title Act 1994*, a community title scheme is created. Community title schemes allow you to own part of a building and share common areas with other owners and occupiers. The body corporate or owners' corporation is funded by the owners of strata-titled property, who pay regular contributions. This rate is generally agreed upon at the AGM. The money goes towards the administration fund (used for the ongoing maintenance of all common areas – cleaning and insurance are examples of items paid for with the administration fund) and the sinking fund (assigned for future capital expenses such as painting, roof repairs, lift maintenance and any major improvements).

Depending on the value of the sinking fund, your contributions may need to increase if major capital works are needed, which can hurt your cash flow. My advice is not to take the agent's word for anything related to the body corporate – always get a second opinion.

Furthermore, be aware that developments with recreational areas incur higher body corporate fees. The basic rule is that the larger or more varied the recreational facilities, the higher the contribution. Having said that, you're entitled to claim depreciation on all common areas, including the recreational facilities. The larger the development and the more extensive the recreational areas, the greater the depreciation benefits.

The body corporate is obligated to hold public liability and building insurance for all common areas. This may extend to some areas of your lot, but not all. For example, if a storm causes water damage to the internal walls and ceiling of your apartment, it is the body corporate's insurance that is likely to be liable, but damage to items such as carpet or furniture would be covered by your insurance policy.

A stand-alone property means no body corporate fees and more freedom to make decisions. But that doesn't mean a freestanding house won't incur maintenance expenses – some of which can be unexpected or urgent – and you may have to organise the repairs yourself.

Here are the key items to take note of in a body corporate report:

- **Financial position:** Body corporates don't trade or invest – their only source of funding is the levy paid by each of the lot owners. The report will provide details of the administration and sinking funds, which will show you how healthy the surplus is for the size of the building, or if there are any arrears. It will also note any big future expenses or levies that would be required on the property.

- **Building defects:** All buildings have some form of defect. Most are usually minor and cosmetic, but some buildings can have major structural defects that affect the tenants' enjoyment of their property and become a major financial drain. It's vital to be aware of any already discovered defects on the common property. The report can show regular maintenance issues that are problematic.

- **Disputes:** Body corporates often have disputes – between fellow lot owners, with the strata committee, with the property management, with contractors and with other parties. Mostly these disputes are minor, but sometimes they become devastating for the entire body corporate and can lead to major financial losses.

- **Compliance with legislation:** Legislation on body corporates is complex and far-reaching, and non-compliance can lead to significant problems and losses.

- **Management issues:** Body corporate management is a complex interchange between a third-party company and the owners, and there can be breakdowns in communication and leadership issues. Infighting is not uncommon, nor is lack of any leadership at all. Poor management leads to an inability to resolve other issues, so it's particularly important.

- **Certificate of currency:** A certificate of currency is issued by your insurance provider to confirm that the insurance policy on the property is effective and valid. It usually specifies the conditions of the insurance, including the policy type held, the premium paid and the date the policy expires. It's essential your property is insured for the correct amount to avoid penalties for underinsurance in the instance of a claim. For instance, if you were to insure the building for 80 per cent of the property's replacement value, the insurer would give you only 80 per cent of your insured value – not the replacement value – in the event of damage, because it's insuring the percentage of risk.

You need to ensure that the property is adequately insured for more than or equal to the replacement value to avoid losses should anything occur. It's also worth checking the insurance cover for specific perils such as bushfire, landslide and hail, as they're not always included as standard. The public liability limit should also be appropriate for the exposure related to the occupancy of the building. A certificate of currency will usually be required to obtain finance.

Note also that body corporate property insurance is not landlord insurance – you will be required to have both.

Property research

Understanding the property is just as important as understanding the broader region to ensure you don't buy a lemon that either falls apart or ends up costing you a fortune. It can be tricky, though, as some properties may appear sturdy on the outside but hide a litany of failures within.

Once you've signed a contract, it can be too late to take it back if you discover something that could affect the property. By doing your due diligence before you sign, you'll protect yourself from any costly headaches.

Caveat emptor

You may have heard the expression 'caveat emptor'; it means 'let the buyer beware'. Basically, when it comes to purchasing property, the vendor is not under any obligation to tell you about hidden or patent defects in the building. You take the building as is, whether it has issues or not. If you sign an unconditional contract, you're locked in – which is why the building and pest report is so important.

When it comes to buying flats and apartments, you'll need to check whether there are any special rules, fees, sinking funds or future maintenance and litigation costs to be aware of.

To help check things that relate specifically to a property you're interested in, ask about:

- the property's title
- the pool certificate and adequate pool fencing, if applicable
- planning schemes, which affect how the property is zoned
- overlays, such as flood or bushfire zones – check there are no 'hidden' restrictions or standards
- unapproved structures or rooms (for example, a garage conversion)
- council approval history, and proposed or granted planning permits
- builders' warranties
- heritage protection
- land boundaries – make sure you are measuring actual fences to ensure the boundaries match
- easements such as sewage and water lines, and shared driveways

- future development potential, either on the property or to the surrounding blocks
- earth resource activity – for example, if the site has mining or quarrying activity nearby
- soil and groundwater contamination, which may prevent future development on the site
- connections for water, sewerage, electricity, gas, telephone and internet – these may not all be connected and so can incur costs to connect.

If you're looking at a renovation down the track, it's also a good idea to look at general access to the property. You'll want to be able to get services, trucks and construction gear onto the site easily, and traffic, roadworks, clearways and tight, one-way streets can add delays and cost to your build.

The contract of sale will go a long way to answering some of these issues, so make sure you request this first and read it thoroughly. A lawyer or conveyancer can help you understand the contract properly and ensure everything is in order.

CHAPTER TWENTY-SEVEN
BUILDING AND PEST INSPECTIONS

To mitigate some of the unforeseen pitfalls your property research may uncover, I advise you to always do a building and pest inspection. It's all well and good to see the property with your own eyes, but an independent inspection is done coldly, dispassionately and by someone much more involved in the technical side of the property rather than the emotional side.

It's important to inspect the physical building so you can see the quality of the construction, its condition, and its susceptibility to pests. When inspecting, take time to discover if there are any potential issues that could arise, especially ones that may be seasonal or intermittent, which the building and pest inspector may not be aware of. Some examples of things to check include:

- poor drainage of the common areas during heavy rain periods
- mould issues due to poor light and ventilation
- cracking due to heat
- inadequate heating or cooling, or boiler issues
- all roof space, underfloor space, the roof exterior and the actual site of the property

- cracks in walls, rust, dampness, mould or leak stains
- functionality of windows and doors
- potential plumbing or electrical issues
- rotting timber and pests
- significant structural movement, major water penetration and considerable deterioration in the building elements, including roofing, rendering and painting.

Serious faults to look out for include:

- unhealthy mould
- poor electrical wiring
- rusting that causes structural integrity to be compromised
- decks, pergolas, sheds, extensions or stairs that haven't been built to code specifications, or aren't registered or approved by council
- structural movement of the building
- roof issues requiring a roof replacement.

It's advisable to take lots of photos and videos inside and outside so you have a reference if an issue arises with a tenant in the future. Make sure you view the whole building, no matter how much inconvenience it may cause to the tenant. This includes storage rooms and parking areas.

Engaging a qualified professional

After your initial inspection of the property, the next step is to have a qualified building and pest inspector formally inspect the building. These inspections can be performed once the property is under contract if there's a building and pest clause or a due diligence clause in the contract. It's essential the inspector is experienced, because anything missed can be very expensive. An experienced inspector will also be able to give you estimates of how much items will cost to be fixed. It is worth noting that the inspectors do not guarantee the quality of the property – they only report on their findings.

The benefit of an inspection is that it allows you to pull out of the deal or renegotiate if you're unsatisfied with its findings. If you buy the property 'conditionally', this means that your purchase can only go ahead conditional to a satisfactory inspection, potentially saving you from buying a dodgy home. If your building inspector is in and out in 15 minutes, they probably haven't done a thorough job, unless there was an obvious, disastrous fault they could see from the outset.

If the property is one you know you'll be completely renovating then it may still be a viable purchase, but you should try to negotiate a lower price if the issues were unknown to you. If you decide to go ahead with some building changes, add a buffer zone to the estimate that the builder has come back with, which will stop you from going over budget when rectifying the situation.

When requesting the building and pest report, you can word the contract specifically to state that if the report shows major structural defects and the vendor is not prepared to rectify them, the buyer can withdraw from the contract. As mentioned, too, in some circumstances you can secure the property's contract subject to a building and pest clause (and a finance clause to allow you to also get approval for finance).

How much?

Building and pest inspectors usually charge between $500 and $1,400 for a standard inspection. Even if you're an experienced builder and renovator, having a third-party inspection can be helpful in negotiations, as the inspector's report will bear more weight than your observations. It's best to book the inspection towards the end of the due diligence process so you don't incur that cost if you don't go ahead with the purchase for other reasons. Most building inspectors will also perform pest inspections.

As for who pays for the inspection, the owner obtains it and can pass it on to any buyer who wants it, but it's not third-party usable – in other words, the buyers have to take it at face value and believe that it is an accurate report. However, you can request a report that's transferable to the buyer. In this case, the buyer pays a small fee towards the inspection. The inspector acknowledges who the new buyer is and that they are buying the property on the basis that the report is true and correct, and if the inspector has missed anything, their insurance can cover the cost of any repairs.

PART VI
CONVEYANCING, FINANCE AND BUYING STRUCTURES

You've done the hard work on your property and analysing the location, but that's only part of the process. Now let's look at the legal and financial aspects of property purchases. Conveyancing, choosing and obtaining finance, and deciding on the right ownership structure for your investments all require careful consideration if you're to achieve the best possible investment outcome.

CHAPTER TWENTY-EIGHT
CONVEYANCING

The main purpose of the conveyancing process is to transfer the legal title or ownership of the property from one party to another. The process usually starts from the time you enter into your contract (the date of the contract) and continues through to the settlement of the purchase. The conveyancing work is performed by a solicitor or conveyancer: a solicitor is a legally trained professional, while a conveyancer has been taught conveyancing but isn't trained in law.

The solicitor or conveyancer you choose needs to be well versed in the laws of the state or territory in which they work, as there are many differences among the states and territories. Look for someone who's highly experienced, not just the person with the cheapest rates. The settlement process can be messy, so you need someone who's confident in what they do and will have your best interests at heart.

Once you and the seller have agreed on all the terms of the contract and signed it, the contract will be dated on the date the last person signed. This is known as 'exchanging contracts', or the property being 'under contract', depending on the state or territory. The contract is legally binding after it's been signed by both parties. The deposit is usually paid before the buyer signs, but in some states and territories (such as Queensland), it can be done after signing, as specified in the contract. The amount of deposit is negotiated between the parties through the sales agent and is paid to the agent as the stakeholder, either on signing or on another date as agreed between the parties.

The contract will contain conditions that the buyer needs to satisfy, including due diligence, finance approval, and building and pest inspections. The period between the signing of the contract and satisfaction of these clauses is known as 'conditional'; once the clauses are satisfied, the contract becomes 'unconditional', and the buyer and seller must proceed to settlement.

During the due diligence period, your solicitor or conveyancer will undertake pre-purchase searches and enquiries. These include checks with government and non-government authorities to ensure there are no outstanding interests or problems with the property. Some of these searches can be performed after the contract is unconditional if they will not affect the outcome of the sale.

The list of searches that can be undertaken is extensive, so it's best to discuss with your solicitor or conveyancer which are appropriate for your transaction, because the costs can add up quickly. The most common are:

- title search
- registered plan
- local authority rates search
- special water-meter reading
- land tax search
- transport and main roads search
- priority notice (if required).

Your solicitor can also arrange an inspection of the body corporate records (also known as a strata report), but many other companies can do this work. This report needs to be obtained and reviewed before going unconditional on a contract.

Once the contract becomes unconditional, a settlement date is booked with all parties (including any outgoing or incoming lenders). Before settlement day, any special conditions – such as repairs or removal of items left at the property – must be satisfied; this is usually checked through a pre-settlement inspection.

For settlement to occur, all parties, including the banks, must be ready to settle. Transfer documents must be signed and returned and stamp duty paid if it's a paper settlement, or all matters completed on PEXA, the e-conveyance platform for Property Exchange Australia. The parties' respective solicitors or conveyancers will prepare the transfer documents, arrange for the seller to organise the release of the mortgage (if there is one) and liaise with the banks to prepare for settlement.

Before settlement, the solicitors or conveyancers will ensure all documents have been prepared and executed correctly, settlement figures have been adjusted accurately and everything necessary has been completed.

On settlement day, the parties' solicitors or conveyancers and their bank representatives will be present for the buyer to pay the balance of the purchase price in exchange for the title transfer and release of the mortgage. If the seller has a mortgage, the seller will give their bank's representative a cheque (or certified electronic transfer) to pay out this mortgage in exchange for its release.

After settlement, the solicitor or conveyancer will contact the seller's real estate agent, authorising the release of the keys to the buyer and the deposit to the seller.

If the buyer has obtained finance from a lender, the lender will attend to the registration of the transfer, the release of mortgage (if any) and registration of the buyer's mortgage with the land registry services. If the property is being bought with cash, the buyer's solicitor will attend to the registration of the requisite documents. If the transaction was performed through PEXA, payment of the purchase price and registration of the transfer, release of the seller's mortgage and registration of the buyer's mortgage will occur immediately online.

Once settlement has occurred, the buyer becomes the legal owner of the property, and the seller is released from any further obligations for payment of rates or taxes – these become the buyer's responsibility. The lender will usually hold the title of the property until the loan is paid off.

CHAPTER TWENTY-NINE
FINANCE

Finance is a hugely important piece of the puzzle. It's commonly known as the hardest part of modern-day property investing. Balancing equity and borrowing power is the key to success in the wake of responsible lending laws. So, while you can leave the execution to your expert team members involved in your property investment transactions, a thorough understanding of what's involved on the finance front will be hugely beneficial to you to expand your portfolio.

Common finance terms

The banking, insurance and superannuation industry in Australia is supervised by APRA. As part of their objective to promote financial system stability in Australia, they are now limiting borrowing capacity, as well as targeting interest-only (IO) loans to protect investors from over-leveraging. This means you might have additional hurdles to jump to secure your finance.

Therefore, don't trust websites with the lowest interest rates, as they can come with catches – some cheap interest rates will restrict you from releasing equity, for example. Instead, use an offset account that lets you save interest on the additional repayments and will give you equity sitting in your account.

In finance, there are a few acronyms to get your head around. Let's look at a few of the main ones.

LMI

Lenders mortgage insurance (LMI) is an insurance you'll need to pay if you borrow more than 80 per cent of your home's value. We looked at LMI in chapter 11, but to recap, LMI protects the lender – not the borrower – but it allows you to get into a property without having such a large deposit. It can be avoided altogether if you have a guarantor.

LMI is lender-specific and not portable. This means that if you decide to refinance to a different home loan and are still borrowing above 80 per cent of the property's value, you will most likely have to pay LMI again. This can often outweigh the benefits of refinancing to a lower-rate home loan. However, you also need to work out the opportunity cost of not utilising LMI and waiting to save up a 20 per cent deposit instead.

For example, if you buy a property worth $400,000 and borrow $360,000 (90 per cent of the property's value), you will pay approximately $7,056 in LMI fees excluding stamp duty. Borrowing 88 per cent is generally a sweet spot between maintaining borrowing capacity and keeping the LMI fees low (half of what they would be at 90 per cent).

LVR

Loan to value ratio (LVR) shows the value of your home loan as a percentage of the property's value. The lower the LVR, the lower the risk you pose to the bank. Some lenders will reward you for having a larger deposit with lower interest rates, higher ongoing discounts and better package deals.

Conversely, lenders consider loans with an LVR over 80 per cent of the property value to be a higher risk. Having a high LVR means you're borrowing a lot more of your home's value. That can leave you vulnerable to rising interest rates and market movements leaving you overexposed.

HEM

The banks use something called 'household expenditure measure' (HEM) to estimate your annual living expenses when considering home loan applications and whether you can afford a home loan. Absolute basics (such as food and utilities) will be factored in, as well as discretionary basics, such as takeaway food, and then non-basics, such as luxury services and holidays.

Borrowing capacity

Affordability and serviceability are two different things – the bank stress-tests loans at higher interest rates than are available at the time – so it's a good idea to understand how the bank calculates both to get your finance approved.

Banks will look at your income, expenses and rental return from the property to determine how much you can borrow. A general rule is that you can borrow around six times your income, but not all forms of income are treated equally by lenders. If you are self-employed or working on a casual or contract basis, most lenders will treat your income as being more subject to variance than that of permanent, full-time wage earners. However, some banks will allow full income to be used from self-employed companies plus their associated addbacks, and some banks will even work from one year's worth of financials.

Most lenders will load up your expenses using a minimum benchmark – even if you are living with your parents rent-free, they will use still use their minimum expense. Have a close look at how much you are spending regularly and try to decrease some of the non-essential luxuries, such as bought lunches or $6 coffees every morning.

Credit card debt or lines of credit will significantly hurt your capacity to borrow. My tip is to close credit cards or reduce their limits, because even if the credit card has $0 outstanding, the bank will act as if you owe the full amount to reduce their risk. Also, avoid any personal or car loans! Banks look at how much debt you're servicing, and this will count as a black mark against you. Also, these loans could potentially reduce your credit rating.

It's well worth finding a good broker who can potentially help you prepare or structure your finances before submission, or at least can identify ways within your finance submission to condition the closure of cards or lines of credit if it helps your application.

The banks also assess the term of the loan and how long you will take to pay it off. If you are paying IO repayments at 4.5 per cent on your loan, the lender may assess your serviceability based on if you were paying both interest and principal repayments at an interest rate 1 to 1.5 per cent higher. They will also typically reduce the rent by approximately 20 per cent to allow for vacancy periods to see if you can service the loan.

Risk ratings

You may not be approved for a loan if the risk rating is too high for the bank. There are also a few other factors to keep in mind that the bank will assess to approve your loan:

- **Location:** Is the property situated on a busy road or beside a noisy facility (such as a train station or factory)?
- **Land:** Is it usable and appealing as a site? Is topography or drainage a challenge?
- **Environmental issues:** Is it in a flood zone, or are there fire hazards?
- **Value:** Is it in an area that banks expect to drop in value over the next two or three years?
- **Square metreage:** Smaller properties, such as apartments under a certain size, can be considered high-risk.

Borrowing calculations

There are two important borrowing calculations to be aware of:

1. **Debt service ratio:** This is the ratio of your loan repayments to your gross income. For most lenders, this figure should not exceed 30 per cent for singles and 40 per cent for couples.

2. **Net debt to income ratio:** This is the ratio of your net disposable income to total debt commitments. For most lenders, this ratio must be greater than 1.25:1 – that is, your net disposable income needs to be at least 25 per cent higher than your total debt commitments.

How to borrow more

There are two ways you can borrow more: increase your cash flow or reduce your outgoings. Increase your cash flow by earning more income (strive for pay rises or get a second stable job), increasing rents on existing properties in your portfolio or pursuing higher-yielding properties. Reduce your outgoings by cutting down on lifestyle costs (such as rent, entertainment and luxuries) and getting rid of credit cards and other liabilities.

The vast majority of lenders will prefer you to pay principal and interest (P&I) on all your loans, as the banks will most often service your debts over a 30-year term. If you take five years IO, the bank will determine your servicing capacity over only a 25-year term, as you effectively have less time to pay the same amount of debt – you lose 5 years in IO payments not amortising the debts. It will obviously impact your borrowing capacity if the bank is servicing your debts over 25 years instead of 30.

A good broker will list your borrowing options from the hardest lenders to get approved with down to the easiest (generally non-bank lenders). They may even know certain lending tricks; for example, some lenders will allow you to take out an IO loan and borrow the difference between P&I and IO, which could potentially give you another few hundred thousand dollars to play with!

Pre-approval

A pre-approval means you have your finances in order but doesn't mean you have the ability to borrow what you like. Let me make this clear: pre-approval on a loan isn't a guarantee that the bank is going to loan you that amount. The bank has to deem the property a safe investment for themselves before you get the green light.

It's a way for a lender to help you and a seller estimate what you can afford. It allows you to know your maximum available funds so you can narrow your search, negotiate with more certainty and, if you're going to auction, bid with more confidence.

However, having several pre-approvals in a short period can potentially harm your ability to borrow, as pre-approvals will be visible on your credit file as loan enquiries, and having many in quick succession and with multiple lenders might create the impression that you're financially unstable. Also keep in mind that if the property is in a certain postcode, lenders may require a higher LVR, which can impact your borrowing capacity.

Here are some things you can do to help your chances:

- Limit your debt on credit cards (such as through buying furniture and accessories for the new home), as this may be seen as a red flag by the lender.
- Maintain both your income and expenditure during the review period.
- Ensure the property you intend to buy meets the lender's criteria and is of equal or greater value than what you are paying for it.

Refinance

A refinance essentially involves entering into a new loan agreement, which you can do with your existing lender (called an 'internal refinance') or with a new lender (an 'external refinance').

Restructuring your loan repayments, how your loans are secured, loan terms and so on can provide substantial financial benefits. The most obvious is that you can lock in a better interest rate, but other good options include resetting your interest-only term and resetting your loan term to 30 years. You may receive a higher variable rate discount or be offered the lowest fixed interest rates.

While each bank will have a different borrowing capacity for different client scenarios (and these policies can change over time), it's not uncommon for a valuation of the same property by two different banks (the valuations from different banks are done by independent third-party valuers) to differ by $50,000. Therefore, my advice is to refinance every two to four years. There is a lot of paperwork involved, but it's worth it in the end.

Refinancing to build a portfolio

If you have equity in your first property, you can extract it to fund another one. This equity could come from you paying down the debt on the property or the property's increase in value.

Your first step is to find a great mortgage broker and organise the refinance of the first property to fund the second. This loan should be pre-approved before you purchase the next property.

Typically, if you have the serviceability and at least 25 per cent equity, you can draw 80 per cent of this (to keep, say, an 80 per cent loan), which will then provide a 20 per cent deposit.

Debt

It's important not to fear 'good debt', although you should be cautious about 'bad debt':

- **Bad debt** includes car loans, credit cards, home loans against owner-occupied properties (these can be good investments providing strong capital growth, but they're considered a liability for lending) and debt against liabilities that depreciate.

- **Good debt** is debt against property, investments, collectables or assets that appreciate in value.

You might obtain loans from banks, loan institutions, money partners, joint ventures or family members. Much like negotiating property prices, it's possible to negotiate loans. There are typically three options when obtaining finance for a residential property:

1. obtain finance from a lender with whom you have already done business
2. investigate the mortgage market on your own
3. engage a broker to investigate the market for you.

1. Using an existing lender

Most people who obtain finance from an existing lender do so for one of two reasons: either they trust and are loyal to their existing lender, or they want to avoid the paperwork involved in going somewhere else for a loan. This method is advisable only if the existing lender is giving you a competitive rate. If you're going to lose thousands of dollars, it's worth reassessing your loyalty!

You won't know if you have the best rate if you don't compare rates from different lenders. A broker will usually be able to tell you quickly if there are more competitive rates, so it's definitely worth at least speaking to one. Sometimes they'll even suggest that you negotiate a lower rate with your existing lender.

Going with an existing lender can also cap your borrowing because it rules out second-tier lenders (smaller banks or non-bank lenders).

2. Investigating on your own

Investigating your finance options takes quite a lot of knowledge and time. You need to know each lender's servicing criteria, fees, offers and conditions, and you'll normally need the details of the property you're buying (or a sample property) to find out what each lender will offer. You then need to submit applications with all the necessary documents and follow the transaction through.

3. Engaging a mortgage broker

Mortgage brokers will compare multiple lenders for you and find the most competitive rates and conditions. Obtaining a loan this way takes much less time and effort than investigating on your own and ensures that you're aware of the variety of options to choose from.

Mortgage brokers

A mortgage broker's job is to work through the types of loans, features and options available to you. They will go directly to multiple lenders and assess the criteria from each institution. These criteria can relate to your ability to service the loan, the interest rate, the loan term and fees, principal-and-interest loans versus interest-only loans, and the use of offset accounts. The broker will help you compare and choose the right loan for your circumstances and plans, and guide you through the loan application process; they will also advocate for you if things go wrong with a lender or mortgage application. They will work with major banks and non-bank lenders, depending on which suits your needs, and find you the best rate – but in the end, it's your decision which lender to go with.

Most people engage a mortgage broker because they do all the work for you and don't charge you – they're paid by the lender once a loan is obtained. Their service is usually uncompromised, nonetheless, as most lenders will pay the broker a similar amount.

A broker will typically look at more than 20 lenders, which individual investors usually don't have the skills or time to do. As they don't get paid unless they obtain a loan for you, in effect, all this upfront work is unpaid. This motivates them to find the best offer for you. Once you have the offer, you can check individual lenders' websites and comparison websites to see if it's competitive.

The interest rate should not be the sole factor determining your decision. Flexibility and loan features aligned with your personal circumstances, investment goals and risk profile are far more valuable to you. With hundreds of lenders all offering different products, an experienced broker can be invaluable.

Note that you should engage a broker only at the stage of making a loan application. It's best to use only one reputable broker, as you don't want them stepping on each other's toes; also, if a lender has enquiries from two brokers about the same property, it can raise red flags. You can speak with multiple brokers initially to find the one you will go with, however. Once you find a good broker, it's worth being loyal to them to achieve a good long-term outcome.

However, not all mortgage brokers are trustworthy or competent. So how do you find a good broker? Using the techniques outlined in chapter 19, once you have the names of a few brokers, meet with them and ask the following questions; consider their answers and check the references they provide, then make your choice:

- What are your qualifications?
- How long have you been a broker?
- How many residential loans have you sourced?
- How many lenders do you have access to?
- What makes you choose one lender over another?
- Do you have three recent clients you can provide as references?

CHAPTER THIRTY

TYPES OF LENDERS AND LOANS

Residential property loans are typically transacted by the major banks, but there are other options available, and they can differ dramatically in the way they operate.

Types of lenders

Let's take a closer look at the different types of lenders and loans to choose from.

Major banks

Major banks are the most common type of lender and the type most people are familiar with. They are often called 'Tier 1' lenders and are regulated by APRA. They offer the advantage of a big branch network, though internet banking has made this less important for many people. Banks are generally owned by shareholders and are usually listed on the stock exchange.

Mutuals

Building societies and credit unions fall under the banner of 'mutuals', as they are owned by members, not shareholders.

They are often called 'Tier 2' lenders and are regulated by APRA and the Australian Securities and Investments Commission (ASIC). The major difference between credit unions and building societies on the one hand and banks on the other is that with mutuals, the profits are reinvested for the members, whereas with banks the profits are for the benefit of their shareholders. Members of mutuals own their credit union or building society, whereas customers of banks are not shareholders. Members of mutuals may therefore benefit from enhanced services, and also lower interest rates and fees in some instances. Most mutual clients feel a sense of loyalty towards building societies and credit unions because they receive more personalised attention.

Mutuals offer a range of financial services and products, including home loans, personal and car loans, credit cards, and savings and everyday transactional accounts. Although they have a different ownership structure to that of a conventional bank, they are still authorised deposit-taking institutions and are regulated by APRA to the same extent the banks are.

Private funders

Private funders (or lenders) are often a conglomerate of wealthy people who pool their money to lend funds at premium rates. Private lenders often have a greater risk appetite; however, this generally means high interest rates and establishment fees. These lenders will be more focused on security than your ability to service the loan, and more interested in the quality of the property and tenant when determining the loan amount.

Private funders are usually lenders of last resort because their fees are high, but they are a fast-growing avenue for developers and investors. Because their loans are not covered by the *National Consumer Credit Protection Act 2009*, they can be a lot easier and faster to obtain.

Advantages of being comfortable with non-banks

A non-bank lender is a lender who doesn't hold a banking licence – that is, they use their own money. They usually come in the form of a building society or credit union, as explained earlier. A lot of people assume that smaller lenders will not be as safe as the big banks. However, all financial institutions in Australia are regulated by independent government bodies, so smaller lenders are just as safe.

Non-bank lenders provide several benefits. Their competitive rates mean they can provide solutions for borrowers who don't meet standard bank lending criteria (such as if they've maxed out their borrowing cap). Some non-banks can lend up to nine times your income, compared to six times from a bank. Also, if your home loan needs a manual credit assessment rather than an automated process, then it's likely a second-tier lender will offer a better option.

APRA supervises all banks, credit unions, building societies and so on in Australia without exception, and has minimum standards which are applicable across the board. The Big Four banks have shareholder interests that may drive a lower risk appetite for lending; they have also been burnt in the past and received large fines and sanctions for poor lending practices.

Types of loans

It's crucial you choose the right loan type for your investment. Most residential loans are over a period of 20 to 30 years and include either principal and interest (P&I) or interest only (IO). Let's look at each different type of loan.

Fixed versus variable interest rates

On most loan types, lenders may offer loans with fixed interest rates or variable rates. Fixed rates enable you to lock in your interest rate (and therefore your loan repayments) for a set period, usually one to five years. During this time, your interest rate will remain the same, regardless of any changes to the official cash rate. The rate of a fixed-rate loan will be higher than that of a variable loan at the time you take up the loan, but if interest rates rise, you'll be financially better off. When the fixed term ends, the interest rate reverts to a variable rate. If you pay out the fixed rate early there may be financial penalties from the lender.

Variable rates are more flexible: loans with variable rates generally allow you to make extra repayments and also to redraw on the repayments. If interest rates go up, however, you may be in a worse position than if you had a fixed rate. Extracting equity to grow your portfolio is possible under variable loans but not fixed loans.

Principal-and-interest versus interest-only loans

Principal-and-interest loans are the most common type for everyday investors. With these loans, you gradually reduce the amount of money you owe by paying off a portion of the principal each month. The monthly repayment is thus higher than it would be for an equivalent interest-only loan.

Interest-only loans, however, are more popular for residential property investors, as they're more tax-effective and will increase a portfolio's cash flow due to the lower repayments. No principal is paid off the loan during the loan term – which is usually three to five years – only the interest on the borrowings. Once the loan's term is completed, it will revert to a principal and interest loan unless the property is refinanced. Some investors opt for IO loans and then deposit the excess into their offset account for future deposits or investment opportunities.

Full documentation, low documentation and no documentation loans

The full documentation (or 'full doc') loan is the most common type of mortgage issued by Australian lenders. You will have to provide more information for this than for any other loan application, including details of your income, asset base, outgoings and debts.

If you're self-employed, a contractor or even a professional investor, it's usually more difficult to provide all the financial documents necessary to satisfy the lender's requirements, so you might pursue a low documentation ('low doc') or no documentation ('no doc') loan. Low doc and no doc loans were very popular before the Global Financial Crisis (GFC) but are now less common. They require less information about your assets and liabilities; the rules are more relaxed compared with a full doc loan. The lender will mitigate this risk by requiring a larger deposit (usually a minimum of 35 per cent) and require a higher rate.

No doc and low doc loans aren't normally designed to be in place for a long period of time: they will usually have a term of six months to three years and then their interest rate will increase. The lenders want to know you have an exit plan to repay the loan.

Lines of credit

A line of credit allows you to use equity from your PPOR or investment properties (both commercial and residential properties are acceptable). It's an ongoing agreement between you and your bank that gives you access to a predetermined amount of credit whenever you need it. With a line-of-credit mortgage, the money you borrow is usually secured against your equity in that property. It functions in a similar way to a credit card: you have a pre-approved credit limit and can borrow as much of this as you want, paying interest on the outstanding balance.

If you're using another property as security against the line of credit, you present a lower risk to the lender and will generally pay a lower interest rate than on other forms of debt. However, because one of your properties is being used as equity for another, if your investments go down in value you may lose both properties.

Note that a line of credit is not amortised – that is, your regular payments don't reduce or pay off the debt.

Split loans

A split loan has two accounts that attract different interest rates; you can allocate as much as you want to each account, as long as it's allowed by your lender. A split loan has two components: a portion that a fixed interest rate applies to and another portion to which a variable rate applies. This allows you to manage the risk of interest-rate fluctuations in times of economic uncertainty in the fixed component and, at the same time, take advantage if rates drop with the variable component.

CHAPTER THIRTY-ONE
THE LOAN PROCESS

Once the contract of sale is signed, it's sent to the broker or lender so they can begin processing your loan. Finance approval is typically the most stressful part of the property purchase, and sometimes extensions of time are needed. Lenders often respond slowly, give poor valuations and require you to submit a large number of documents, mostly in hard copy. Valuations can also be unpredictable due to the difficulty in finding comparable properties. The larger your portfolio, the more complicated the lending and valuation procedure becomes.

If the contract is subject to finance, you'll be trying to obtain finance at the same time as being under contract. It's critical that your mortgage broker and lender have all the information they need from the start of the process, including proof of your personal information and financial history.

Your personal information

A formal proof of identification check may be required if you haven't borrowed from a particular lender before. This can usually be organised at your local post office and may require you to present your passport, driver's licence, birth certificate, and government identification cards such as your Medicare card.

You will also need to give details about the length of time you have been at your current address, information about the number and ages of any dependants you have (children or otherwise) and your relationship status, as your partner may also be responsible for the loan.

Your financial situation

Lenders will look at your banking history. Ideally, to maximise your chances, you'll have had stable and regular income and expenses for at least two years. It's fairly obvious that you should try to avoid unpaid debts, bankruptcies and legal monetary matters that would affect your capacity to service a new loan.

You'll need to supply information about your finances, which may include details of:

- your assets, including proof of your savings history, your bank accounts, current properties and any other investments (such as shares)

- your living expenses and outgoings

- your credit, store and charge cards, including statements

- any history of defaults or arrears

- proof of employment

- proof of income and government payments

- bank statements showing income up to six months back

- group certificates, tax returns, tax assessment notices and balance sheets for the most recent financial year

- your partner's liabilities.

If you're struggling to obtain finance, as a last resort you can request an extension of the finance period under contract. Many agents and sellers understand the harsh lending environment and will usually agree when given a valid reason.

The five Cs of credit

It's also a good idea to consider the 'five Cs of credit': character, capacity, capital, collateral and conditions. Lenders use this analysis to determine the risk associated with a loan.

Character

Lenders want to know if you – the borrower – and any guarantors are honest and have integrity. Character in this context amounts to your willingness to pay back the mortgage. The lender needs to be confident you have the background, education and stability of employment to do this, and will also verify whether you have a criminal record. Banks will sometimes give better rates or higher LVRs to people in certain professions – usually white-collar or government jobs that are stable and provide a lower risk of unemployment.

A lender will examine the personal credit of all borrowers and guarantors involved and will want to ensure that your past financial information is sound and regular. If you have any delinquencies, be prepared to explain them.

Capacity

Capacity means serviceability, or your ability to repay a loan. Lenders base their assessment of your capacity on a number of factors, including your income, the loan amount, your age, and your other commitments and expenses. The bank uses these factors to calculate a debt service ratio (DSR), which is the percentage of your monthly income expected to be spent on debts. The bank will want the DSR to be below a specific number, which will vary among lenders.

When considering your income, the lender will take into account factors such as overtime, commissions and company cars. Depending on your profession and how frequent your overtime is, though, the bank may take only a portion of it into its calculations.

There are restrictions about counting income from a second job: you'll need to have been receiving this income for a certain period before it can be included, and each lender has its own criteria to determine how much of this income will be counted. Your service-ability and how much you can borrow will therefore be heavily dependent on your choice of lender.

Lenders will generally consider only a portion of the rental income you receive from a property portfolio, and will take into account the strength of the lease, the property's location and vacancy rates. This allows a buffer for any vacancy periods you may experience and is known by lenders as 'shading the property'.

Lenders will also calculate repayments by adding a margin interest-rate percentage (2.5 per cent or more) to the variable rate. This 'assessment rate' is used to predict whether you'd be able to meet repayments if there were an interest-rate rise.

Your regular and irregular outgoings will be considered as well, of course. These include regular expenses, credit-card debts (and their limits), car loans, student loans and the number of children or dependants living in your home. These can all negatively affect your loan serviceability and make it much harder to obtain finance. To increase your chances, it's essential to minimise the limits on all credit cards and always pay any personal and car loans on time.

Capital

Capital represents the wealth of the borrower(s) and any assets or valuables that make up their total net worth. In short, it's the value of your assets minus your liabilities. The lender considers your savings, investments such as real estate and shares, the value of your car and other assets, minus any personal loans and credit card and other debts. Lenders would like to see that you have a buffer that would allow you to keep paying your loan if you had a financial setback, such as losing your job. By looking at your capital, lenders assess your ability and willingness to save and accumulate assets and then compare this with your age.

Collateral

Collateral is an important consideration, but its significance varies between different types of loan. Generally speaking, collateral is represented by the properties used to secure the loan. If you are cross-collateralising – using another property as security to obtain the loan – and are unable to make the agreed repayments, the bank has the right to seize your property to repay the debt. However, before they do this, they usually explore all other avenues, including reducing or freezing the repayments for a period. If the lender does end up selling your property, you retain any capital gains from the sale.

If you can't provide collateral or security in the form of property, some lenders offer guarantor loans, which use a third party's collateral as a backup.

Conditions

'Conditions' refers to the financial conditions at the time you submit your application – specifically your interest rate, principal amount and general market conditions. It encompasses any outside circumstances that may affect your financial situation and ability to make loan repayments.

Lenders may evaluate the overall business climate, both within your industry and in associated industries, and the economic conditions that could affect your borrowing, including the Reserve Bank's cash rate and any policy changes that affect borrowers' ability to borrow money. These factors can affect the lender's allowable LVR on the property.

Valuations

Once the finance application has started, lenders will perform a valuation. There are three main ways banks value your property:

1. **Desktop valuation or automated valuation model (AVM):** a report from a data provider such as CoreLogic
2. **Kerbside valuation:** a valuer parks outside your property and values your property from the kerb
3. **Full valuation:** a certified valuer visits your property to carry out a full valuation.

A desktop valuation is an automated computer valuation done using property data, recent comparable sales and property listings. As the name suggests, the valuation of the property can be estimated from a desk, without needing a valuer to physically visit the property. It is automatically generated, instant and cheaper than a full valuation.

It is considered reliable when:

- the property in question has been sold in the last ten years
- the property is in reasonable condition
- the property has not been substantially changed (built, subdivided or renovated) since last sale
- the property is relatively standard (normal size, normal building)
- there are many similar properties sold or listed in the local area.

These are considered unreliable and a kerbside or full valuation is ordered if:

- the property was last sold 20-plus years ago
- the property has been substantially changed since last sold (otherwise a desktop valuation may come in lower than a full valuation if it's not taking improvements into account)

- the property is unusual, such as if its best use is as a development site, it has a granny flat at the back or it is a display home
- there are few local sales available for comparison.

Desktop valuations also provide a risk analysis. They tell the lender how much to trust the figure reached. If the desktop valuation report's risk score is too high, a lender may order a full valuation instead.

You cannot request the type of valuation you would like – you can only choose the lender. If a desktop valuation comes in low, you can request that the lender does a full valuation or explore another lender. Different lenders will quite often value properties differently, so it is worth the investigation. Desktop valuations are typically only valid for 90 days, whereas a full valuation is usually valid for three to six months.

Under-market valuations are common, because valuers take a very cautious approach. If the valuation does not come back as you expected, you can renegotiate the purchase price, request a full valuation, try another lender or walk away from the deal. If you do renegotiate the property price because of a poor valuation, you need to analyse carefully why the banks valued it lower than you expected. You can also pay the difference to get the deal done if you think it's a good property.

If more time is needed, you can ask for an extension of finance – but if the extension is denied, you then need to terminate the contract to avoid penalties. Usually, the seller will give you a few days' extension, sometimes a couple of weeks if they really want the sale to go ahead as soon as possible. They can even give you a conditional extension that enables them to advertise or go under contract with another buyer if you don't respond in time.

Importantly, though, don't be afraid to walk away if you can potentially not complete the sale or it's just not working. As I've said before, the costs you've spent on the deal up to this point are insignificant compared with those of having a property that doesn't suit your needs.

If everything does check out and the valuation is acceptable, you can satisfy the contract's financing condition. However, it is only recommended to go unconditional on the contract after due diligence and building and pest inspections are complete.

Before settlement day, your conveyancer will outline the funds available for settlement to occur and will work with the lender to ensure a smooth transfer of registrations. The lender will attend to the registration of the transfer (either physically or online through PEXA), the release of the mortgage (if any) and registration of the loan with the land registry services. The lender usually holds the property's title until the loan is paid off.

CHAPTER THIRTY-TWO

BUYING STRUCTURES AND SYNDICATES

Deciding on the best ownership structure for your property invest-ment can be a confusing and complex process. However, it's vital to get right, because it can save you thousands of dollars in tax and also protect your personal assets in the event of bankruptcy.

Here are the popular tax structures available to invest in property:

- individual ownership in your name
- joint tenancy
- tenancy in common
- joint venture
- trust (family discretionary trust or unit trust)
- self-managed superannuation fund (SMSF)
- company
- syndicate.

Individual ownership

Investing in your own name is the simplest and most common method – it has no set-up cost and minimal compliance is required.

One of the benefits of individual ownership is that you can negatively gear the property if there are any losses. However, if the property is positively geared, this may not be particularly beneficial: the positive cash flow is added onto your salary, which would cause some people to have to pay much more tax.

On the downside, you could lose the property if you become bankrupt, even if your debts don't relate to the property.

Individual ownership is suitable for inexperienced property investors and for those who aren't concerned about the risk of bankruptcy.

Joint tenancy

When two or more people own a property as joint tenants, each 'joint tenant' owns an interest in the whole of the property. This means that each joint tenant is entitled to possession and enjoyment of the whole of the property, and therefore cannot exclude any other joint tenant from any part of the property.

Joint tenancies are subject to a right of survivorship, which means that upon the death of one joint tenant, the surviving joint tenant inherits the interest of the deceased joint tenant. For example, if there are two joint tenants, then upon the death of one joint tenant, the surviving joint tenant would own the property in full and the joint tenancy would cease. However, if there are three joint tenants and one of the joint tenants dies, then the two remaining tenants would continue to own the property as joint tenants.

Joint tenancy is a common form of ownership among couples and people who make equal contributions to the purchase of the property.

Tenancy in common

Under a tenancy in common, each 'tenant in common' is regarded as having a separate and undivided interest in the property, equivalent to the percentage of the property that they hold. Tenants in common may hold their shares equally or otherwise in unequal portions. A tenancy in common is not subject to a right of survivorship, and it is therefore important when holding a property as a tenant in common that your interest in that property has been dealt with in your will.

This is a common form of ownership where the purchasers of a property make unequal contributions to the purchase price. This form of ownership is also often used to assist with estate planning when an owner does not wish for their interest in the property to automatically go to the remaining owner (or owners) when they die.

Joint venture

A joint venture involves two or more individuals buying the property – they may be friends, family members or business partners. With this structure, in effect, you're entering a long-term relationship with the other person, and this needs to be clearly understood between the parties. It's important, therefore, to put all the terms of agreement in writing to avoid any possible legal difficulties later. Having an exit strategy is also vital, as individuals' circumstances can change dramatically over time, both financially and personally.

If possible, it's preferable to set up separate loans for each joint buyer. This means that if your partner struggles to make payments or defaults on their loan, it won't affect your borrowing capacity or credit history. Even if the joint venture runs smoothly, individual loans are beneficial, because if you want to borrow to invest in something separately in the future, only your portion of the first loan will count against your ability to service a second loan. Without separate loans, the entire debt will count, even though someone else is paying half of it.

When you're buying as part of a group, it's essential that there's a consensus about how the property will be treated over time and the exit strategy. All members of the group need to have the same goals – whether to, for instance:

- sell the property in a short time, or hold it long term
- maximise the LVR in order to hold less capital in the deal, or maintain a modest LVR to maximise cash flow
- refinance the property at the earliest opportunity, or pay down the loan over time
- add value to the property by injecting capital, or spend less to have a higher short-term cash flow.

Some members may have a stable job and lifestyle; others may need to extract cash or sell for personal reasons. Others may not be able to get finance alone, and this may affect their goals for the investment. It's important that each member of the venture spells out their goals, and it's advisable for a contract to then be drawn up for the group to ensure everyone is protected legally.

Trust

Essentially, trusts are designed to provide the investors with distribution income from the property during the lifetime of the trust. However, distributions are not guaranteed, nor is the return of initial capital invested. Your best bet is to obtain advice from an accountant who is a property tax expert before you make an offer to buy a property.

Trusts are used for risk mitigation and asset protection (protecting personal assets and debt from acquisition), estate planning (saving on fees, taxes and costs associated with death), and tax savings (nominating trust beneficiaries a percentage of the profits).

The person who creates the trust (a lawyer or accountant) is called the 'settlor'. The settlor generally has no involvement in the operation of the trust after it's established – they simply create it. The trustee makes the decisions; the person (or often company) who is the legal owner of the trust is in control of the trust. There's also the appointor or principal, who is the person who has the power to appoint, remove or replace the trustee. Finally, there are the beneficiaries, who are the beneficial owners of the trust property. Often the trust deed will name one or two individuals, and the rest of the beneficiaries will be defined by their relationship with those people.

This trust structure is illustrated in Figure 3.

Figure 3: Trust structure

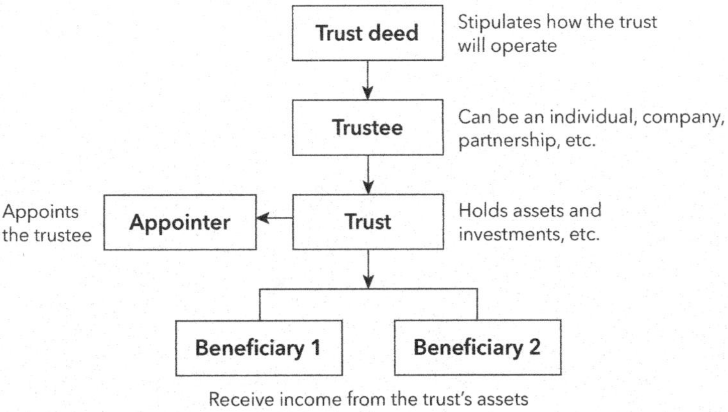

| Trust deed | Stipulates how the trust will operate |

| Trustee | Can be an individual, company, partnership, etc. |

Appoints the trustee — Appointer ← Trust — Holds assets and investments, etc.

Beneficiary 1 — Beneficiary 2

Receive income from the trust's assets

Family discretionary trust

Holding a property in a family discretionary trust can be beneficial, as you don't need to specify the share of each spouse and family member – rather, you have the flexibility to distribute income in the most tax-effective manner from year to year. A trust also protects assets (especially when you have a company as a trustee) and allows you to carry out estate and succession planning. Trusts are eligible for a 50 per cent discount on capital gains tax, as well.

The negative aspects of family discretionary trusts are that they cost quite a lot to set up, they have a higher compliance cost for tax returns, and you can't distribute losses – which means they aren't suitable for holding negatively geared properties.

Family trusts can also attract stamp duty, with the cost varying between different states and territories as shown in Table 10.

Table 10: Stamp duty costs for family trusts by state/territory

State/Territory	Cost
ACT	Nil
NSW	$500 (due 3 months from the date of deed)
NT	$20 (due 60 days from the date of deed)
Qld	Nil
SA	Nil
Tas.	$20 (due 3 months from the date of deed)
Vic.	$200 (due 30 days from the date of deed)
WA	Nil

Unit trust

Unit trusts differ from other trust structures in that the trustee divides the trust's property into fixed and quantifiable parts called 'units'. Beneficiaries subscribe to these units in a similar way to shareholders subscribing to shares in a company. Unit trusts provide the investors – 'unit holders' – with certainty, as the money or property from the trust is distributed to the beneficiaries in fixed proportions according to the number of units they hold. For this reason, unit trusts are more appropriate than discretionary trusts when third parties who are not family members are investing together.

The other benefits of a unit trust include asset protection (especially when you have a company as a trustee), estate and succession planning, and being eligible for a 50 per cent discount on capital gains tax.

Self-managed superannuation fund

Self-managed superannuation funds (SMSFs) are used when an individual wants to take full control of their superannuation assets. Setting up an SMSF is costly, however, and takes a great deal of preparation, and managing it requires ongoing attention to ensure the many regulations are met.

Some of the tax benefits are as follows:

- Once the individual or individuals retire, they pay no capital gains tax.
- Loan repayments can, in effect, become tax-deductible (provided members salary-sacrifice).
- Income (after expenses and any capital gains on the disposal of property) is taxed at a maximum rate of 15 per cent, compared with the up to 46.5 per cent that a regular investor could be paying.
- Employer superannuation contributions can be used to help repay any loan associated with the property, and can be protected against general debt recovery and bankruptcy proceedings.

One point to note is that any tenants you have in an SMSF property must be third-party and not related to you.

Company

A company is a legal entity in its own right; when you borrow in the name of a company, it will own the investment property. The company will be the borrower and all directors of the company will be required to guarantee the loan.

Some of the benefits of buying under a company structure are a lower tax rate, the ability to plan tax through dividends, the fact that the tax paid by the company can be franked – that is, passed on as credit to shareholders with dividends – and that it provides a much higher level of protection for your assets outside the company.

However, financing is usually harder for companies to obtain due to banking restrictions, and you risk losing the property if your company is sued.

Some other drawbacks are that the set-up and maintenance costs of a company structure are quite high, and companies aren't eligible for the 50 per cent discount on capital gains available to trusts and individuals. A company cannot distribute losses either, so this isn't a suitable structure if your property is negatively geared. Another issue is that, although you won't be personally liable for the company's debts as a director, you will be legally obligated for responsibilities such as ensuring solvent trading (in other words, for ensuring the company doesn't trade while insolvent).

Syndicate

Property syndicates pool funds from many investors to acquire a property for the financial benefit of all. They offer qualifying 'sophisticated investors' the opportunity to part-own high-quality, expensive residential or commercial real estate that would ordinarily be beyond their reach. Syndicates also enable the investor to be more passive – that is, less involved with the tenancies and management of the property.

The term 'sophisticated investor' is defined in the *Corporations Act 2001* and denotes a professional investor, so this isn't an ownership structure that's available to beginner investors or those on lower incomes. To qualify as a sophisticated investor, you'll need a signed confirmation from your accountant (in the form of a sophisticated investor certificate) that you own assets of more than $2.5 million or earned more than $250,000 in each of the previous two financial years. If you invest $500,000 or more in a syndicated offering, however, you're not required to provide a sophisticated investor certificate.

A syndicate is legally structured as a unit trust, with investors applying for ordinary units in the trust. In many respects, a unit trust is similar to a company: as mentioned earlier, units have most of the same characteristics as company shares. However, syndicates are usually established for a finite period – generally about five years – after which it is intended (but not mandated) that the asset be sold. Syndicates will guarantee ordinary unit holders the right to cash out their investment after five years, whether or not the property is sold at that time. The trustee has the right to sell the property and wind up the trust before five years if it considers that to be in the best interests of unit holders.

The syndicate trust's formation and management are delegated to an associated company, which handles finding the property (or properties) and negotiating the purchase; performing due diligence on the properties; organising financing arrangements; maintaining all financial records; dealing with real estate agents, property managers, tenants and maintenance contractors; and the day-to-day running of affairs.

Note that the operators of the syndicate are required to hold an Australian Financial Services Licence (AFSL), which imposes comprehensive and strenuous obligations on the licensee. The principals of the licensee must possess extensive relevant experience and the appropriate degree of expertise. Licenses are tightly regulated, and the company will be audited annually, with the auditors certifying that the company is complying with all of its legal and statutory obligations. The affairs and finances of each unit trust the licensee manages are also audited individually every year.

As with other trusts, an agreement governs the relationship between all parties and stipulates key terms and conditions. A regularly used term in the agreement for syndicates is the 'objective', which identifies the reasons for creating the property syndicate. The goals are typically shared across the group.

In summary, for the right investor, a syndicate is a way to invest in many properties without owning them completely, and to purchase expensive large-scale residential properties that would otherwise be out of reach. Some syndicates are organised privately between investors, but there are companies that will organise syndicates.

The benefits of syndicates include the following:

- **Less capital required:** Individual investors are able to buy higher-valued properties with less capital, as there are multiple investors.
- **Diversification:** Having a smaller outlay by being part of a syndicate allows you to spread the risk over multiple properties.
- **Stable returns:** By diversifying your assets, you're able to regulate your returns and have less volatility.
- **Time saving:** Investing in a syndicate requires less effort than finding and securing a property yourself, and you'll spend less time on management and administrative matters.

The risks of investing in a syndicate include the following:

- **Less control:** Since there will be multiple investors, you have less say in decisions.
- **Other vested interests and transparency:** The financial interests, goals and wishes of the other investors need to be taken into account. They can sometimes have hidden intentions, however, and it's important to acknowledge that other investors' goals and personal and financial situations may change.
- **Management issues:** Investing in a syndicate leaves control in the hands of a management team, and this requires a level of trust. Seeking regular updates from the team will help to avoid potential issues, however.

PART VII
GROWING YOUR PORTFOLIO AND VALUE-ADDING

I f you've made it this far, well done! For me, this next part is the most exciting and rewarding part of residential property investing. You've expended the time and energy to purchase and set up your property using the right structure with the right team; now you're ready to move into a strategic position to grow your portfolio over the long term.

There are many factors that affect the way property grows, but basically it all comes down to the levers you can apply that affect two key elements: capital growth and return from cash flow.

Capital growth and the return from the cash flow are fundamental when it comes to expanding your portfolio. However, the most powerful part of property investing is that you can put a 10 to 20 per cent deposit on an asset while receiving benefits on the full amount of the asset (after paying around 2 or 3 per cent interest on the remaining debt). For example, if you pay a 20 per cent deposit on a $1 million property – so, $200,000 – and the property value increases by 10 per cent, the return would be $100,000 – that's a 50 per cent cash return!

There is always a huge debate in the industry about buying a capital growth property versus a cash flow property, and it's a topic that I talk about a lot. The best way to look at it is this: which property will help you achieve your goals?

To illustrate, you'll see in Table 11 on the next page that I compare two $1 million properties. The first is a typical 'blue-chip' negatively geared property, while the second is a higher-cash-flow property. Let's assume the capital growth property has 6 per cent capital growth and the cash flow property has 4 per cent. Ignore rental increases, taxes and all the other variables – this is purely illustrative!

Table 11: Blue-chip property versus cash flow property

Capital growth	Blue-chip property		Cash flow property	
	6%	Cash flow	4%	Cash flow
Year 1	$1,000,000	-$10,000	$1,000,000	$5,000
Year 2	$1,060,000	-$10,000	$1,040,000	$5,000
Year 3	$1,123,600	-$10,000	$1,081,600	$5,000
Year 4	$1,191,016	-$10,000	$1,124,864	$5,000
Year 5	$1,262,477	-$10,000	$1,169,859	$5,000
Year 6	$1,338,226	-$10,000	$1,216,653	$5,000
Year 7	$1,418,519	-$10,000	$1,265,319	$5,000
Year 8	$1,503,630	-$10,000	$1,315,932	$5,000
Year 9	$1,593,848	-$10,000	$1,368,569	$5,000
Year 10	$1,689,479	-$10,000	$1,423,312	$5,000
Profit	$689,479	-$100,000	$423,312	$50,000
Total profit		$589,479		$473,312

At first glance, you can see that after ten years you would have made approximately $100,000 more from the blue-chip property. Looks good, right? Stay with me, however, because there's a bit more to it. The cash flow property would have been taking less money out of your pocket each year, which gives you options. You may be able to buy another property sooner; plus, you will also typically have a better serviceability with lenders and be able to borrow more should you wish to buy future properties. In addition, you will be able to live off the passive income from this property, whereas you would need to sell the blue-chip to realise the value. My point is that a deeper understanding of how investing works will always help you in the long run.

If you're wondering whether you should wait years to save up for a deposit or jump in sooner, consider that property values often increase at a far faster rate than you are able to physically save your cash. There's always plenty of talk around the barbeque about waiting for prices to drop, but the reality is that borrowing can be great, so don't be fearful – it's best to buy an investment property today rather than having to wait years to save up. Property is a long-term game; with this mindset, the second-best time to invest is now, with the best time having been ten years ago.

The following chapters cover several tactics for investing in residential property – which are right for you depends on where you are now and where you want to be tomorrow. Plus, there's also the best part: our 15-year property plan. Let's take a look!

CHAPTER THIRTY-THREE
GROWING YOUR PORTFOLIO

Leveraging

One of the best ways to expand your portfolio quickly comes down to the basics of leveraging – compounding, specifically. Compound returns occur when you earn a return on an investment and then reinvest those proceeds, thereby increasing your earning power. In other words, if you earn a percentage income on the capital you've invested, that income is then added to the amount you began with so you can earn a percentage income on that as well, earning 'income on the income'. Thus, the total amount you're earning income from increases, and this accelerates the growth over time.

For example, if you invest $100,000 at a 7 per cent per annum interest rate, and it's compounded monthly, in ten years you'll end up with $200,966 – as you can see in Figure 4, overleaf.

There's a quote commonly attributed to Albert Einstein that goes, 'Compound interest is the eighth wonder of the world. He who understands it, earns it; he who doesn't, pays it'.

Leveraging is fantastic as it allows you to purchase more properties – and higher-quality properties – than you could otherwise afford. It is also an example of 'good debt', which we covered in chapter 29, but to recap: good debt generates an income and should be tied to an asset that appreciates in time, whereas bad debt doesn't generate an income and doesn't have a good chance of appreciating over time.

Real estate is one of the few investments that lenders will let you leverage significantly, and when you combine compound returns with leveraging, you can achieve growth on a much larger scale than with other assets. You can generate a very high cash-on-cash return.

It's worth noting again that you need to beware of the potential negative effects of leveraging, though. Be cautious about taking on large amounts of debt – while the positive returns can be great, you'll also magnify any losses. Maintaining a comfortable LVR is crucial for portfolio risk mitigation. For the most part, lenders are likely to keep you in check, but this isn't always the case with private lenders or vendor finance. Therefore, ensure you have a good mortgage broker to help you.

Figure 4: Investing $100,000 at 7 per cent per annum for 10 years

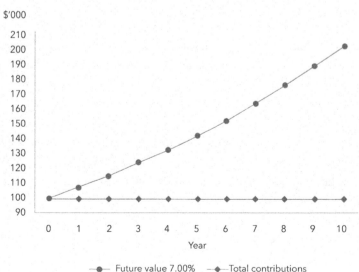

When deciding how much to leverage, you'll need to consider a number of factors, including the following:

- **Your risk appetite:** How much money can you risk? How many dependants and commitments do you have? Ask yourself how much cash or equity you need and how aggressive you want to be with your investing. If you're a high-income earner with a large amount of liquid savings, for example, you can take on more risk than a low-income earner with minimal savings.

- **Your goals:** Developing a strategy will come down to your individual short-term, medium-term and long-term goals. I spoke about goals in the introduction to this book – remember, your goals should be based on what truly makes you happy. Don't chase a particular passive income amount or number of assets for the sake of it: be realistic about what you want and what you're prepared to sacrifice to achieve it.

- **Your time frame and exit strategy:** It's important to consider your time horizon – the period in which you would like to expand the portfolio to achieve your desired cash flow. Also think about your exit strategy. Will you need to sell one or more properties to obtain cash or to pay off a PPOR at some point?

Remember, a property's performance and the market conditions may not live up to your expectations, so purchase each property with a margin of safety. Not every property in your portfolio will be an outstanding performer – there are too many market variables to get everything right in the long term, although focusing on getting as many fundamentals right as possible will minimise this risk. It's also essential to stress-test your portfolio. This involves checking how your portfolio would perform at higher interest rates or with periods of vacancy, and ensuring that you can financially handle these situations.

One of the most common mistakes investors make is not having sufficient cash reserves for unexpected expenses. If or when a property becomes vacant, you need a buffer to be able to pay the rates, mortgage, maintenance bills and any other expenses. Choose a buffer amount that's appropriate for you, taking into account your risk profile, how many properties you own, your responsibilities, your income and the typical vacancy rate of the properties in your portfolio.

Interest only versus principal and interest

The interest-only (IO) strategy involves adjusting your loan to only pay the interest, rather than paying off the principal and interest (P&I). The lower repayments during the interest-only period could help you save more or pay off other, more expensive debts. This strategy may be useful for short-term loans, such as bridging finance or a construction loan. Also, for an investment property you could claim higher tax deductions, because you'll have a larger debt on the property and hence more interest payable in the long term.

Another benefit of this strategy is that inflation naturally erodes value of the debt, making it worth less over time. Let me give you an example. Say you purchase a $500,000 property on a 90 per cent loan, which equates to $450,000 debt. In ten years, the asset appreciates to $1m but your debt remains the same, $450,000. That $450,000 hasn't had inflation applied to it, so is naturally worth less than it was ten years prior – people's incomes and value of money will have increased due to inflation.

A downside of the IO strategy is that the interest rate could be higher than on a P&I loan. You pay more over the life of the loan. You also pay nothing off the principal during the interest-only period, so the amount borrowed doesn't reduce. In addition, your repayments will increase after the IO period, which may not be affordable.

If your property doesn't increase in value during the IO period, you won't build up any equity. This can put you at risk if there's a market downturn, or if your circumstances change and you want to sell.

Rentvesting

Rentvesting is a strategy that has been gaining popularity over the past few years. It's where you rent somewhere you like – somewhere with lifestyle appeal, perhaps, or a quick commute to work – while leasing your investment property and using the debt to make money (leveraging).

It's a good strategy if you find yourself priced out of your desired area and unable to buy a PPOR, or if there are better growth regions than your desired area. Furthermore, it enables you to get onto the property ladder without having to wait longer for your dream home. The trick is to invest the difference – the 'spare' money made from renting rather than buying in your lifestyle location – rather than spending it. This strategy is also better suited to those on a higher income – because earning more generally results in a higher borrowing power – and when there's a big difference between what it costs to buy and rent in the same area.

On the negative side, renting means you won't be able to make any changes to the property you live in unless you have approval from the landlord. Plus, you'll miss out on full capital gains tax exemptions (to fund your next purchase) if you sell your investment property.

Buying a principal place of residence first

As an investment strategy, purchasing your principal place of residence (PPOR) is a great way to start out. Firstly, you're entitled to First Home Owner Grants and stamp duty savings, plus you'll save capital gains tax (CGT) if you sell because you live in the property versus renting it out as an investment.

If you do decide to sell, the tax savings of selling your PPOR over an investment are huge. You can continue treating your former home as your main residence for CGT purposes even though you no longer live in it.

To be eligible for the CGT exemption, the property must:

- have been your main residence first – you cannot apply the main residence exemption to a period before a property first becomes your main residence
- have stopped being your actual main residence – that is, you stopped living in it.

If the property was continuously your main residence, the usual rules for the main residence exemption apply. This means if you use it to produce income, such as rent, you will be entitled to only a partial main residence exemption from CGT.

If you are a foreign resident when a CGT event happens to your residential property in Australia – for example, you sell it – you are no longer entitled to claim the main residence exemption.

Usually, a property stops being your main residence when you stop living in it. However, for CGT purposes you can continue treating a property as your main residence for up to 6 years after you move out if it is used to produce income, such as rent (sometimes called the 'six-year rule'), or indefinitely if it is not used to produce income.

During the time that you treat the property as your main residence, it continues to be exempt from CGT to the same extent that it was exempt when you stopped living in it – even if you start renting it out after you leave – and you cannot treat any other property as your main residence (except for up to 6 months if you are moving house).

PPOR ownership in a low-interest-rate environment can be cheaper than renting, allowing you to save the free cash flow and pay down your debt faster, then refinance into an investment property later.

You'll have security in that the landlord can't pull the rug out from under your feet because they decide to sell, and you won't have to worry about the 'dead money' of renting if you are not investing elsewhere. Also, PPORs are generally in suburbs with lifestyle appeal and strong demand, which pushes prices up and drives strong capital growth (although this also means the barrier for entry into the market is high).

However, if you max out your borrowing capacity too early on by purchasing a PPOR property, you may not be able to purchase a future investment property due to lack of serviceability. There's also another argument that because you're paying to live there, it's a money taker, not a money maker.

If where you want to live is at the end of a property cycle, it could be quite some time before you see capital growth. If you are looking to build an investment property portfolio, getting short-term and medium-term capital growth will enable you to grow your portfolio more quickly.

Investment property

Purchasing an investment property can get you into the property market sooner than waiting for your dream PPOR, and when rented out, the tenants may cover all expenses (providing cash flow every week). If you purchase an investment property, you'll also be eligible for significant tax savings, such as negative gearing, depreciation and maintenance costs. As we covered earlier, the key difference between an investment property and a PPOR is that an investment property is driven by financial needs, rather than emotional or personal requirements. Assessing numbers and data will be your best friend, rather than getting bogged down looking at aesthetics and the 'feel' of a place.

Refinancing

Refinancing is a fundamental part of all of my property plans. You'll see in my 15-year property plan that I have refinanced each property every year or two, which enables me to find a lower interest rate with other lending competitors. In turn, this reduces the loan terms and enables the loan to be paid down faster, should this be your strategy.

Refinancing could also help you buy an investment property potentially even without a deposit. That's because many lenders will let you use the equity you have in your property as security against another property. You can also draw on your equity in the property to renovate or develop the property. By refinancing, you could give yourself the chance to roll these into the one debt secured against your property (potentially at a lower interest rate).

It's worth noting that refinancing involves a lot of paperwork and time. Many people don't refinance for this reason alone, but for me, it's a no-brainer: it's definitely worth it when you are able to free up your cash and reduce your yearly repayments that otherwise would have been going straight to the bank.

Value-adding

Value-adding is all about creating equity faster. It's about applying the right levers to the right property to meet your wealth objectives more quickly, and understanding what will work to deliver you the best outcomes. It's a great way to ensure you always make money, even if the suburb where your investment property is located doesn't perform how you thought it would, leading to bad capital growth.

After value-adding, you can refinance the manufactured equity into a second property, which is the first step to building a large portfolio with a limited initial pot of cash and getting a high return of capital due to leveraging and refinancing.

The next few chapters cover some value-adding options.

A 15-year property plan

Let's look at a property plan to see how you can build your portfolio, with real numbers and realistic outcomes. Table 12, overleaf, shows a 15-year plan, with a goal to own five properties worth a total of $12.5 million, as well as total cash flow (or passive income) of $100,000 per year. With this plan, if you start with a $1 million property, you'll end up with a $12.5 million portfolio. It may look like a lot of numbers and data, but there's really nothing complicated in there – I've used very simple mathematics. It is designed to be something that you can achieve, rather than so many of the 'pie in the sky' plans you read about in the newspapers every weekend.

Before I show you the table, I've made some basic assumptions:

- The table assumes you have no serviceability issues. For many people, this can often be the reason why you can't follow a plan, but I am presuming that over 15 years your income will increase, and that will increase your serviceability. If your individual circumstances change and you need to alter your plan, you can switch to higher-cash-flow properties (such commercial, in which case I invite you to read my other book, *Commercial Property Investing Explained Simply*) or perform value-add equity projects such as renovations, developments or even joint ventures.

- Every property buy-in assumes a 4 per cent rental yield.

- The plan includes 5 per cent rental increases per year, because rents typically double every 15 years.

- The plan doesn't account for personal circumstances and factors outside your control that can speed up or slow down the process.

- Each additional property will have 25 per cent upfront costs: a 20 per cent deposit, plus an extra 5 per cent to allow for purchasing costs such as stamp duty, conveyancing fees and other acquisition costs.

- The plan does not take into account major renovations such as new kitchens or bathrooms.

- Tax on the positively geared nature of the portfolio is ignored.

- All properties are on IO loans. The additional savings of $30,000 per year could represent the principal payment, SMSF contributions or payments to accelerate portfolio growth. One possible strategy could be to switch to P&I repayments at year 15 and pay loans off over the next 15 years to prepare for retirement.

Table 12: 15-year residential property plan

Capital growth rate	6% per annum
Rental increases	5% per annum
Interest rate	3.5% per annum
Rental yield at purchase	4%
Loan type	Interest only
Rental management	7% per annum
Depreciation benefit back at tax time	$1,000 per annum
Repairs	$1,000 per annum
Insurance, water bills, land rates, etc.	$4,800 per annum

Stamp duty	3.5% of purchase price
Additional savings	$30,000 per annum
First property deposit required	$250,000 (including 20% deposit, stamp duty, building and pest inspection, conveyancing fees, etc.)

Now, take a look at Table 13, overleaf. Your starting point will be the acquisition costs required for your first property of $1 million, which I've calculated at $250,000. As mentioned, this includes a 20 per cent deposit, plus 5 per cent for upfront costs including stamp duty, building and pest inspections, and conveyancing fees; and you can draw this from savings, refinancing your PPOR, or using other properties in your portfolio. If you really wanted to accelerate the start of your portfolio, you could look at buying two properties on 90 per cent LVR, as you would then have two properties growing instead of one, but you would need to pay LMI.

You'll hold your first property for three years, until you are ready to buy your second, which involves refinancing the first and adding in your cash flow, additional contributions and 80 per cent equity. While you will purchase a property that is less expensive than the first, its value will gradually grow as you buy more expensive properties and your cash flow and equity increase.

To sum up, in 15 years, after buying five properties, you'll create a portfolio size totalling more than $12.5 million with total equity of more than $3.6 million. Not bad going, considering that you don't need to do anything else. Of course, plans like this won't suit everybody, but a portfolio of five properties is more manageable than 30, which other investors are keen to spruik! Huge portfolios in short periods of time are just not possible unless you have a huge income to save the deposits and the serviceability for lenders to give you loans. If it sounds too good to be true, it usually is.

Table 13: 15-year residential property plan figures

Year	Property (refinance)	Purchase price/value	LVR	Loan amount	Weekly rent	Annual rent	Loan interest	All other outgoings	Post-tax cash flow	Accumulated cash flow	Additional contributions	Growth equity	Cash flow + contributions + 80% equity
1	#1	$1,000,000	80%	$800,000	$769	$40,000	$28,000	$8,600	$4,400	$4,400	$30,000	$60,000	
2	#1	$1,060,000	75%	$800,000	$808	$42,000	$28,000	$8,740	$6,260	$10,660	$60,000	$63,600	
3	#1	$1,123,600	71%	$800,000	$848	$44,100	$28,000	$8,887	$8,213	$18,873	$90,000	$67,416	$207,753 used for property #2
4	#1 (1)	$1,191,016	80%	$952,813	$890	$46,305	$33,348	$9,041	$4,915	$4,915	$30,000	$71,461	
	#2	$830,000	80%	$664,000	$638	$33,200	$23,240	$8,124	$2,836	$2,836	$0	$49,800	
5	#1 (1)	$1,262,477	75%	$952,813	$935	$48,620	$33,348	$9,203	$7,068	$11,984	$60,000	$75,749	
	#2	$879,800	75%	$664,000	$670	$34,860	$23,240	$8,240	$4,380	$7,216	$0	$52,788	
6	#1 (1)	$1,338,226	71%	$952,813	$982	$51,051	$33,348	$9,374	$9,329	$21,313	$90,000	$80,294	
	#2	$932,588	71%	$664,000	$704	$36,603	$23,240	$8,362	$6,001	$13,217	$0	$55,955	$324,367 used for property #3
7	#1 (2)	$1,418,519	80%	$1,134,815	$1,031	$53,604	$39,719	$9,552	$5,333	$5,333	$30,000	$85,111	
	#2 (1)	$988,543	80%	$790,835	$739	$38,433	$27,679	$8,490	$3,264	$3,264	$0	$59,313	
	#3	$1,297,000	80%	$1,037,600	$998	$51,880	$36,316	$9,432	$7,132	$7,132	$0	$77,820	
8	#1 (2)	$1,503,630	75%	$1,134,815	$1,082	$56,284	$39,719	$9,740	$7,826	$13,159	$60,000	$90,218	
	#2 (1)	$1,047,856	75%	$790,835	$776	$40,355	$27,679	$8,625	$5,051	$8,314	$0	$62,871	
	#3	$1,374,820	75%	$1,037,600	$1,048	$54,474	$36,316	$9,613	$9,545	$16,677	$0	$82,489	

Year	Property (refinance)	Purchase price/value	LVR	Loan amount	Weekly rent	Annual rent	Loan interest	All other outgoings	Post-tax cash flow	Accumulated cash flow	Additional contributions	Growth equity	Cash flow + contributions + 80% equity
9	#1 (2)	$1,593,848	71%	$1,134,815	$1,137	$59,098	$39,719	$9,937	$10,443	$23,601	$90,000	$95,631	
	#2 (1)	$1,110,727	71%	$790,835	$815	$42,373	$27,679	$8,766	$6,927	$15,242	$0	$66,644	
	#3	$1,457,309	71%	$1,037,600	$1,100	$57,198	$36,316	$9,804	$12,078	$28,755	$0	$87,439	$523,856 used for property #4
10	#1 (3)	$1,689,479	80%	$1,351,583	$1,193	$62,053	$47,305	$10,144	$5,604	$5,604	$30,000	$101,369	
	#2 (2)	$1,177,371	80%	$941,897	$856	$44,491	$32,966	$8,914	$3,610	$3,610	$0	$70,642	
	#3 (1)	$1,544,748	80%	$1,235,798	$1,155	$60,058	$43,253	$10,004	$7,801	$7,801	$0	$92,685	
	#4	$2,095,000	80%	$1,676,000	$1,612	$83,800	$58,660	$11,666	$14,474	$14,474	$0	$125,700	
11	#1 (3)	$1,790,848	75%	$1,351,583	$1,253	$65,156	$47,305	$10,361	$8,489	$14,093	$60,000	$107,451	
	#2 (2)	$1,248,013	75%	$941,897	$898	$46,716	$32,966	$9,070	$5,679	$9,290	$0	$74,881	
	#3 (1)	$1,637,433	75%	$1,235,798	$1,213	$63,060	$43,253	$10,214	$10,593	$18,394	$0	$98,246	
	#4	$2,220,700	75%	$1,676,000	$1,692	$87,990	$58,660	$11,959	$18,371	$32,845	$0	$133,242	
12	#1 (3)	$1,898,299	71%	$1,351,583	$1,316	$68,414	$47,305	$10,589	$11,519	$25,613	$90,000	$113,898	
	#2 (2)	$1,322,894	71%	$941,897	$943	$49,052	$32,966	$9,234	$7,852	$17,141	$0	$79,374	
	#3 (1)	$1,735,679	71%	$1,235,798	$1,273	$66,213	$43,253	$10,435	$13,526	$31,920	$0	$104,141	
	#4	$2,353,942	71%	$1,676,000	$1,777	$92,390	$58,660	$12,267	$22,462	$55,307	$0	$141,237	$863,353 used for property #5
13	#1 (4)	$2,012,196	80%	$1,609,757	$1,381	$71,834	$56,342	$10,828	$5,664	$5,664	$30,000	$120,732	
	#2 (3)	$1,402,268	80%	$1,121,814	$990	$51,504	$39,263	$9,405	$3,835	$3,835	$0	$84,136	

Year	Property (refinance)	Purchase price/value	LVR	Loan amount	Weekly rent	Annual rent	Loan interest	All other outgoings	Post-tax cash flow	Accumulated cash flow	Additional contributions	Growth equity	Cash flow + contributions + 80% equity
13 cont.	#3 (2)	$1,839,819	80%	$1,471,855	$1,337	$69,524	$51,515	$10,667	$8,343	$8,343	$0	$110,389	
	#4 (1)	$2,495,179	80%	$1,996,143	$1,866	$97,009	$69,865	$12,591	$15,553	$15,553	$0	$149,711	
	#5	$3,453,000	80%	$2,762,400	$2,656	$138,120	$96,684	$15,468	$26,968	$26,968	$0	$207,180	
14	#1 (4)	$2,132,928	75%	$1,609,757	$1,450	$75,426	$56,342	$11,080	$9,005	$14,669	$60,000	$127,976	
	#2 (3)	$1,486,404	75%	$1,121,814	$1,040	$54,079	$39,263	$9,586	$6,230	$10,066	$0	$89,184	
	#3 (2)	$1,950,208	75%	$1,471,855	$1,404	$73,000	$51,515	$10,910	$11,575	$19,918	$0	$117,013	
	#4 (1)	$2,644,889	75%	$1,996,143	$1,959	$101,859	$69,865	$12,930	$20,064	$35,618	$0	$158,693	
	#5	$3,660,180	75%	$2,762,400	$2,789	$145,026	$96,684	$15,952	$33,390	$60,358	$0	$219,611	
15	#1 (4)	$2,260,904	71%	$1,609,757	$1,523	$79,197	$56,342	$11,344	$12,512	$27,181	$90,000	$135,654	
	#2 (3)	$1,575,588	71%	$1,121,814	$1,092	$56,783	$39,263	$9,775	$8,745	$18,811	$0	$94,535	
	#3 (2)	$2,067,221	71%	$1,471,855	$1,474	$76,650	$51,515	$11,166	$14,970	$34,888	$0	$124,033	
	#4 (1)	$2,803,583	71%	$1,996,143	$2,057	$106,952	$69,865	$13,287	$24,801	$60,418	$0	$168,215	
	#5	$3,879,791	71%	$2,762,400	$2,928	$152,277	$96,684	$16,459	$40,134	$100,492	$0	$232,787	

Portfolio size: **$12,587,086**   Total equity: **$3,625,117**

Total cash flow per annum: **$101,161**

CHAPTER THIRTY-FOUR
RENOVATIONS

For many people, renovating is an easy way to add value to property. Whether your property is a PPOR or an investment, renovating can lift the appeal of a home to make it more rentable, as well as attract future capital growth faster.

How much do you spend? The general rule is to spend no more than 10 per cent of the current market value of the home. The other rule of thumb is that you want to get any money you put into the renovations back twofold.

But what do you renovate, and where do you start? This is where you have plenty of options, such as painting, fittings and other aesthetic work, or more structural work such as adding or removing walls (subject to council approval) and creating space where there previously wasn't.

Ultimately though, renovating is about problem-solving. How do you eliminate buyers' objections? Look closely at your floorplan. If you have a three-bedroom, one-bathroom house, you could transform this into a three-bedroom, two-bathroom house by adding another bathroom as an ensuite within one of the bedrooms. Straight away, you improve the house's liveability and increase the value people are willing to pay without having to extend out or up.

Obviously, money doesn't grow on trees, so there are some good rules around prioritising what renovations to focus on:

- Use colours and designs that appeal to a wide variety of people. Think of your property as a blank canvas, and choose neutral tones that people can add their own personality to. Not everyone will like your passion for bright purple!

- There are some rooms that will always add more value than others if done well. The best are bedrooms, bathrooms and kitchens. Expect to add on value if these spaces are well designed and fitted with quality products and colours.

- You might be able to save some time and money if you ask your property manager for trade references. Many managers have great trade contacts as they often need to source good-quality people for jobs for their rental list.

- If you're indecisive about whether to proceed, look at comparable sales in your suburb or street to see if a renovation is worth it for you.

If you do decide to go through with a renovation, my tip is to pay to stage your property and engage a professional photographer. This will create a higher yield for future leases, and the bank valuer may give you a more generous valuation as well.

Renovations provide several advantages. You can create equity faster, because you can buy an older home for less and be strategic in how you renovate it. They're also a great way to ensure you always make money – if the suburb doesn't perform how you thought it would and the capital growth is low, you'll still raise the value of the property. Some buyers will even pay over market value for older homes with character, such as Queenslanders or Art Deco homes, because of their scarcity.

Renovated properties should also achieve higher yields. They'll attract higher-quality tenants, meaning fewer vacancies and main-tenance issues, and any issues you do have will be easier to track (for example, it's easier to tell if newer furnishings are damaged or carpets stained). Finally, there are many depreciation benefits on renovation improvements, which can save a lot from your tax bill.

However, there are also several potential downsides to renovations. The biggest challenge when renovating is sticking to a strict budget and keeping emotions out of it. I commonly see newer investors get carried away with over-capitalising. Try to follow the rule of focusing on bedrooms, bathrooms and kitchens, and don't deviate!

Another downside is that you might need to rent elsewhere or have the house vacant as the renovations are being completed, which means no rental income, so do your figures to work out what the potential loss may be. If you do remain in the property, you'll have to deal with dust, noise and managing trades coming in and out. Renovating is not for everyone, especially when delays turn weeks into months, so consider your routine and whether you can ride out any hiccups to timelines. Also, with older properties especially, you may find asbestos, mould or termite damage that wasn't evident from the property report, which can eat up your profit as well as your time.

If you do decide to go ahead with a renovation, ensure you get council approval first. Building permits are necessary to ensure your house remodel meets structural and fire safety requirements. Inspectors can make you rip out non-conforming work, which can create a very expensive headache when you're looking to sell your property down the road. So, think ahead to ensure the permit process is followed, and always put in a call to the council to double-check that what you are proposing is permissible.

CHAPTER THIRTY-FIVE
SUBDIVISION

Subdivision involves splitting up land into multiple lots. Drive around any of the suburbs 15 kilometres from the city in Melbourne and you'll see this property strategy in action everywhere.

Subdivisions most commonly involve splitting land into two, but more divisions are possible. They provide the highest and best use of the land in terms of utilising the house-to-land ratio. When you subdivide land, each new lot has its own property record entity, and you must also submit a development application (DA).

If you're going to go ahead with a subdivision, it will need to comply with necessary regulations, including land use and access to roads and utilities. These vary depending on the location. You'll need to use a town planner to help with local regulations and council approvals. And, as always, seek legal and financial advice from professionals before you start. In other words, build your team first to get your ducks lined up.

Subdividing provides some great options. You can either sell the land, build and hold, or build and sell (or a combination of the three). You can increase your cash flow by holding one side (manufactured equity) and selling the other to reduce debt. You can also create equity faster through subdivision than the traditional property strategies, because smaller, separate blocks of land will usually have a higher value per square metre than one large block. Finally, a subdivision isn't reliant on the market to provide capital growth, as you can fabricate the equity uplift in the land by building a separate dwelling on its own title.

However, a subdivision isn't suitable for every situation, and therefore can be a very expensive and unsatisfactory exercise if you get it wrong. You must ensure that you pick the land well, as a starting point, so that you can build good capital growth and ensure you meet council regulations for the subdivision. Doing a subdivision also takes time – there's a lot more paperwork involved than with renovations, and if you don't have the organisation or preparation, you can easily fall behind. You may uncover unpleasant surprises relating to areas such as groundwater and sewerage, too, which may throw out your initial feasibility.

It's worth keeping in mind, as well, that small blocks may not be as attractive to buyers, and therefore may not increase as much in value over time as other developments.

CHAPTER THIRTY-SIX
DEVELOPMENT

Everyone wants to be a property developer, and property development is one of the most common areas I get asked about. While property development can be a highly profitable tool to grow a property portfolio, it is not for the faint-hearted. It is risky, highly time-consuming and can also be very expensive – far from the public perception of rolling up to sites in a sports car with a cafe latte.

Regardless of the property, there are 16 core steps in the property development process. Before you do any of these, you must ensure that you speak openly and honestly with your expert team – and specifically your accountant. You'll need to remember the GST implications as well as working out what the intent of the property is.

Now, let's take a look at the 16 core steps:

1. **Find a site:** There are a few important things you'll need to consider, including the type and scale of the property, the correct legal structure for ownership, the area for your development, interest from local agents and local consultants such as architects and surveyors, and understanding the local real estate market with research. Also, what's your endgame?

2. **Conduct initial due diligence:** This is your first investigation into ensuring the development will work, covering off things like zoning, size of lots (or number of dwellings), yield, services, overlays, site characteristics and any potential obstructions.

3. **Secure the site:** Make sure you create your design, obtain approvals and schedule your builders before you settle for the site. To purchase your site, aim for a win-win in all scenarios through great communication, understanding and being a good listener when negotiating. Ensure your contract is subject to finance.

4. **Conduct advanced due diligence:** This is the in-depth financial feasibility reporting, when you'll look at all expenses and fees, the specific services requirements, reporting obligations (such as air quality or geotechnical), and then searches on the property to cover off any caveats, covenants, easements and any other issues.

5. **Settle on the site:** This is when you ensure all the finances are in order so that there are no hold-ups for your development application process.

6. **Lodge your development application (DA):** This is the formal approval you will need to proceed with your development. You'll need your team members, comprising an architect, town planner, landscape architect, surveyor and civil engineer, who all have to create their own report and plans, with the end goal to design something you want and that the market wants. A DA has a process to follow, too, which includes the following:

    *   **Pre-lodgement:** presenting an assessment-ready application to council explaining your plans for the development and the impacts to your neighbours

- **Lodgement:** includes specialist reports, council's DA form and checklist, all matters required for DA (such as adherence to the Environmental Planning and Assessment Regulation 2021) and the DA fee

- **Assessment:** a formal check from the local council, looking into environmental impacts, access issues, services, objections, and so on (to protect the broader public's interests)

- **The conditions of your consent:** conditions attached to the approval or refusal of your DA (with approval generally lasting for five years), which may require you to make changes such as reducing the height of the dwellings or removing elements

- **Building permit or construction certificate:** required by some states and territories before your builder can commence (post-approval); in other states and territories, it's step 9 (as shown below)

- **Occupation certificate:** authorising the use of the development – without it, you are not allowed to have people living in the property and banks will not settle on the property.

7. **Secure development approval:** This means that you have been given the official and legal green light to progress to the building and construction phase.

8. **Commence pre-selling (if this is your strategy):** It's time to start selling off the plan to acquire cash to build your development. This is when you would engage a marketing agency to put together a campaign for you.

9. **Obtain the building permit or construction certificate:** This approval legally enables you to build on your site and is a major part of the process. For approval, you'll need to include

approved architectural and extensive engineering drawings and plans from a host of engineers, general requirements and National Construction Code (NCC) requirements, and any relevant certificate requirements. You may need demolition permits, operational works permits, and plumbing and drainage approval. Lock everyone into certain time frames and hold them to account!

10. **Tender construction:** Now you're ready to find a builder, and you'll receive offers from construction companies interested in working with you on your project.

11. **Select a builder:** Lock in your builder and make sure you are both happy to proceed, as you'll be working very closely over the rest of the process.

12. **Organise development finance:** This is when you'll need to get your finances lined up and utilise the skill of your bank and brokers to ensure there are no hold-ups. Development finance can differ significantly from traditional finance, and the more feasible the project, the less equity you will need to contribute. Some private lenders will provide the lending based on the completed price of the project (also known as 'gross realisable value').

13. **Commence construction:** The key building works stages are foundation, slab, frame/firewall and completion. Each of these stages will be inspected as part of the building regulations, and the build won't be able to continue without sign-off at each stage.

14. **Complete construction:** The build will hopefully be complete within the allocated time frame, but builds often blow out due to delays caused by material costs and availability, and skills shortages.

15. **Arrange title registration:** This is the formal documentation of ownership of the site with the appropriate register. It describes the land and records the current owner, among other things.

16. **Complete settlements:** You're now a property developer with a successful property under your belt. The settlements are the final payments allocated for each of the properties as part of your development.

To reduce your risk, there are a few things you can do to ensure a smoother process. Firstly, seek advice from a town planner, civil engineer, surveyor, architect and solicitor beforehand, so that you can get a bit of a heads up as to whether your development makes sense. Don't engage in a project that has a high probability of unmitigated major risk occurring. This may completely eat up your profit margin or even put you at a loss. Ensure you structure your projects to keep yourself distanced from any financial fallout if things go wrong. You should also understand what your opportunity is – what problem you are solving – to ensure demand in your project, because if you're not solving a problem, no one will be interested in buying.

Popular property developments

Now let's take a look at two of the most popular property developments: duplex and townhouse developments, and apartment developments.

Duplex and townhouse developments

Duplexes and townhouses have higher land values than apartments, which translates to potentially longer-term growth. They are usually easier to build and a more affordable project to develop compared to a block of apartments, because there are generally fewer individual properties as part of a development and thus fewer fit-outs (bathrooms, kitchens and services). As a result, they can be completed in a shorter time frame. They also have a smaller footprint, which makes them ideal for smaller blocks.

Apartment developments

Apartments have higher profit margins than townhouses because you can sell more on the same block. Once the foundation is built, simply aim high, build up and watch your profits grow! This is why developers will always try to max out the building heights on their developments, because the higher the building, the greater the number of apartments, and the greater the profits.

Having said that, each area has set building heights, and developments can yo-yo between hearings and approvals. The following factors can determine the height and number of apartments permitted:

- site orientation and shadowing on neighbouring properties
- space for cars
- existing windows on the bordering land
- the slope of the land.

Developing apartments is complex and involves a much trickier engineering and construction process, due to the increased level of services and facilities involved. As a result, the construction process is longer, too.

Feasibility

The feasibility stage is the most crucial to complete before you start any development. This will tell you whether what you are proposing will be successful – and profitable – before you commit. During feasibility, you will be able to consider best-case and worst-case scenarios and to build in contingencies to mitigate any unfavourable situations. Basically, the more accurate your feasibility, the more profit you will make. Spend time on this and don't be tempted to cut corners!

There are a few types of feasibility to consider for every project: static, cash flow and market.

Static feasibility

Static feasibility is used in the early stages of a project to see how the financial outcomes look – the gross realisable value. It includes major items that will incur cost or generate revenue for the project, such as the purchase price of the site, closing costs of purchase, holding costs, construction, consultant fees, and so on.

Cash flow feasibility

Cash flow feasibility includes major and minor items, allowing you to project a cost for each of these over a period of time so that you can see what your cash flow position will be every month. It is applied after static feasibility to verify your thoughts and assumptions.

Market feasibility

Here are some questions to ask at the outset to check the market feasibility of your development:

- How can you get to know your area and become a local expert?

- What do raw sites sell for, and what do two- and three-bedroom townhouses sell for?

- What does the market want?

- When you go to inspections and speak with agents, what are people saying they like and don't like?

- Who is your target market, and what are they looking for? Big or compact homes? Standard finishes or optional inclusions? Carpet, tiling or wooden flooring; 20- or 40-millimetre stone benchtops?

- What about amenities? Under-mounted sinks are more expensive; splashbacks, tiles and larger amenities (such as sinks or ovens) will add to your expenses.
- Will you include air conditioning? Throughout the whole house, or just in the living areas?
- What about lighting? Designer or budget, and where?

You want to find the 'sweet spot' between finishing the build to meet market demand and being mindful of not over-capitalising on construction costs to ensure the development is financially feasible.

Each suburb and council has its own set of building guidelines, as well as local rules regarding the safety and comfort of residents. Developments lend themselves to more objections from the local community because of the increase in built form and potential issues to do with overshadowing and overlooking. Town planners can help you understand what's possible and what's not in your particular area, so it's worth making contact and building a relationship. As with all developments, if you allow flexibility in your plan in case things change, you'll have a much smoother process. Keep in mind that developments have longer completion times, which can lead to increased holding costs.

Why do a property development?

Good question! Most people think that property development is too hard and only suitable for professionals. In fact, most don't have the time, knowledge, skills or contacts to become developers. It takes all of those to create a good property development, and sometimes a bit of luck, too.

The benefits of becoming a property developer are all about allowing you to grow your property portfolio faster and more safely than most investors. Yes, there are always two sides to the coin – clearly there are significant potential risks if you get involved in property development – but there are also many upsides.

Here are some of the excellent benefits you can gain from property developing:

- **Savings:** Right from the outset, you can save money. This is because, rather than buying properties at retail, you can acquire your investments at 15 to 20 per cent below their market cost. Why? You don't pay developer's margin, agent's commission, marketing or other costs usually included in the price of buying real estate. This can translate to significant cost savings.

- **Profits:** You're in the game to make a profit, and if you invest at the right time in the property market, you'll be on your way to making good profits selling your development projects.

- **Easier finance:** Once you have completed your development project, you can approach banks to re-mortgage your properties and they will usually lend you 80 per cent of their retail value when completed. In many instances, this will be about what the property cost you pre-development. In other words, it's a bit like borrowing 100 per cent of the cost of the property, or having 'nothing down'.

- **Leverage:** This is one of the clear benefits of property developing – you attract massive leverage when you have completed a development project. Often you control a substantial property or even two or three townhouses with little capital in the properties as equity – because they will be worth more than when you bought them, you will have effectively reduced your LVR.

- **Tax benefits:** As you now own many new properties, you'll receive all the benefits of government incentives and depreciation allowances, which will give you a great after-tax return.

- **Higher rental return:** Your tenants will pay market-rate rents, but the cost of your property was substantially below the retail price. This means your rental yields will be higher than for someone who bought their property at market value.

- **Security:** If you have developed the property correctly and successfully, property development can be very lucrative. If you buy your development site well, your investment will always be underpinned by the security of real estate in a prime position.

CHAPTER THIRTY-SEVEN
SURVIVING A DOWNTURN

You may experience a downturn in your investments for many reasons – it could be the economy, the demand for your type of property, an act of God or because your tenant is struggling. In these circumstances, the ability and value of your property manager – if you're using one – will really shine.

How to protect yourself from risk

There are several ways to protect yourself from risk. First, understand that property is a long-term game. Buy in areas that are high in demand with tightly held supply, so that when it comes time to sell, your property has an active consumer base. Stress-test your portfolio or potential purchase with high interest rates to ensure you will not be in financial stress if rates rise. Engage property professionals – for example, without engaging a building surveyor, you may find termites only after settlement; or without knowledge of the local area, you may not find a tenant for months. Know your local area, or engage a buyer's agent. Also, take out landlord protection insurances.

Diversify your wealth across other investments, such as shares. This can help mitigate the failure of any single asset. For example, if you buy an off-the-plan apartment and the market turns before the apartment is constructed, the value of your property may decrease, and the bank may require a larger deposit, which you may not be able to pay if everything you have has already been sunk into the investment.

Also, consider investing in commercial property as well as residential. There are a range of pros and cons when investing in commercial, but the greatest benefits of commercial real estate are higher rental yields and longer tenancy periods. Depending on your goals and current situation, you could potentially find a property with rental yields larger than the costs of the investment. Commercial property also provides another way of diversifying your assets. For more information, read my other book, *Commercial Property Investing Explained Simply*, which covers commercial property in great detail.

Protecting your properties in trusts

Setting up your property within a trust is another way to protect it from creditors if one of the beneficiaries goes bankrupt or is the subject of legal action. This means that they can't use the property to settle any debt owed. One of the risks of developing property is that business owners, professionals and builders are particularly exposed to litigation as individuals due to the nature of their businesses. Providing guarantees, taking on business debts and legal obligations can result in bankruptcy and the loss of personal assets, but a trust goes a long way towards providing protection against risk.

If you buy with other people, you may decide on a trust structure where each buyer is a member with an allocated share each. If you buy property as part of a business venture, buying in a trust may be preferable to the directors buying in their personal names.

The downsides of a trust are that negative gearing is quarantined within the trust, while other losses are not realised until you sell, which could damage your returns. A good accountant will advise you on whether this is the best course of action for you and help set it up. Revisit chapter 32 for more information on trusts.

Acts of God

Throughout the English-speaking legal world, natural disasters such as earthquakes and tsunamis are referred to as 'acts of God' (or 'force majeure events'). These are circumstances outside anyone's control that could not be foreseen or guarded against. Acts of God may provide a defence or an exception to liability, such as in a situation that would otherwise be a breach of contract or a tort.

Some events commonly classed as acts of God in Australia include floods, cyclones, bushfires and droughts. After COVID-19, legislation was changed to define a pandemic as an act of God, so insurance policies must be checked closely. It's essential to check whether building and landlord insurance will cover these possibilities, depending on the risk in the property's region. This needs to be assessed during the due diligence period before buying a property. You can also consider having a surveyor risk-assess your property and improve its resilience to such an event – for example, by undertaking bushfire-mitigation works on the land surrounding the property.

If your insurance doesn't cover these events, it's important to work with your tenant to ensure an optimal outcome for all.

Global economic crises

As discussed in chapter 18, the economy has quite an impact on property prices and business success, and so a global economic crisis would affect your residential investment property. Depending on your tenant, it may affect their ability to remain in your property.

One of Australia's largest recent recessions occurred across 1990 and 1991 – unemployment rose by about 5 per cent, the Australian share market dropped about 40 per cent, and the worst fall in any capital city was a maximum 2.3 per cent in capital value. Three of the capital cities actually grew in capital value during this time, however, to a maximum of 6.8 per cent!

The Hollywood film *The Big Short* explores the GFC in the US, and it is testament to Australia's banking system that we didn't suffer the same fate. This was because our system is underpinned by responsible lending, which meant that Australia's housing market was largely unaffected by the GFC.

Pandemics

At the time of writing, the COVID-19 pandemic has forced legislation changes in regard to tenants' rights. The pandemic will no doubt change the face of many other regulations as well as the demand for certain property types and locations, as people shift towards larger houses and lifestyle regions.

Again, it's important to work with your tenants during these times and examine any claims they make about income loss, and to see if a rent reduction would be fair. Consider the following steps:

1. **Refer to government incentives:** Some tenants will not be affected by COVID-19 but may still ask the owner for a discount on their rent. In this case, suggest that the tenant explore the government grants available under any stimulus measures in place. This is the first thing to do.

2. **Consider rent deferrals:** Some tenants may ask for their rent to be waived for the period. If rent deferrals are allowed, this will provide the best net return for you.

3. **Consider rent relief:** Rent relief or a discount may turn out to be the best option in the end, as you want your tenant to have the best outcome from a compassionate point of

view. I have always strived to do the right thing over what is technically allowed.

4. **Refer to government legislation:** If the government has enacted legislation – such as a mandatory code of conduct covering how landlords and tenants are to deal with each other in the pandemic – all parties must comply with the legislation. This is designed to protect the landlord, the tenant and the economy.

EPILOGUE

Residential property is a great way to achieve your financial goals and generate a passive income – it can enable you to live the happy life you desire without being tied down to a job! As you can see from the flowchart overleaf, there's quite a lot to know about it.

Whether you're a first-time or experienced property investor, I hope that this book has given you some extra knowledge and confidence with buying residential property.

I wish you all the best in the future – happy investing!

I'd like to finish on a quote that I think is quite fitting to both life and property:

'Service to others is the rent I pay for my room here on earth.'

—Muhammad Ali

The residential property investing process – explained simply

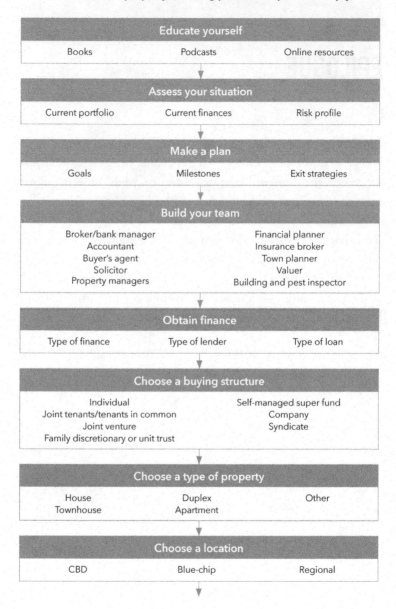

Educate yourself

| Books | Podcasts | Online resources |

Assess your situation

| Current portfolio | Current finances | Risk profile |

Make a plan

| Goals | Milestones | Exit strategies |

Build your team

Broker/bank manager	Financial planner
Accountant	Insurance broker
Buyer's agent	Town planner
Solicitor	Valuer
Property managers	Building and pest inspector

Obtain finance

| Type of finance | Type of lender | Type of loan |

Choose a buying structure

Individual	Self-managed super fund
Joint tenants/tenants in common	Company
Joint venture	Syndicate
Family discretionary or unit trust	

Choose a type of property

| House | Duplex | Other |
| Townhouse | Apartment | |

Choose a location

| CBD | Blue-chip | Regional |

Property acquisition

Search	Building and pest inspection
Negotiate	Lender's valuation
Perform due diligence	Settlement

▼

Post property acquisition

Property management	Tenant lease review
Value-adding	Rent review
Regular portfolio review	

▼

Build and enjoy passive income!

ABOUT THE AUTHOR

Steve Palise has worked for Australia's leading buyer's agencies, executing more than 1,200 property acquisitions for himself and his clients. He has purchased in every capital city and major regional town in Australia.

In this book, as in his work, he draws on the mathematical and analytical skills developed in his previous life as a chartered mechanical and structural design engineer to break down what works best in property. As with engineering, property investment is based primarily on the numbers.

Having acquired an impressive property portfolio that allowed him to leave the workforce sooner rather than later, he's now passionate about helping others to achieve their goals and financial freedom. His philosophy is that investments should increase your wealth and passive income with as little risk as possible.

Steve Palise is a licensed real estate agent experienced in sourcing quality residential and commercial property investments. He has helped thousands of clients secure and purchase properties, and believes property investing should be not only smart, but enjoyable along the way!

CONSULTATION SERVICES

Steve Palise offers buyer's agent services in Australia for nationwide residential and commercial property. Consultation is available for:

- Mentoring
- Portfolio review and strategy design
- Sourcing properties and development sites
- Conducting due diligence on a property
- Settlement process support
- Introduction to property managers, solicitors, insurers, etc.
- Tenant selection

To speak with Steve, or to follow what he has been up to, please visit him online:

- **Website:** www.paliseproperty.com
- **LinkedIn:** www.linkedin.com/in/steve-palise/
- **Facebook:** https://www.facebook.com/paliseproperty

ACKNOWLEDGEMENTS

Putting a book like this together is a team effort, and I'd like to take the opportunity to express my gratitude for those who have made it happen.

Firstly, I'd like to thank the 'book world' experts – Annie Reid from Atrium Media, and Lesley Williams from Major Street Publishing. Thank you for your guidance, experience and support. I look forward to working with you again for another instalment!

Secondly, a special mention goes to Nicholas Cornacchione for his help with the compilation of information for this book. Wishing you all the best with your university studies, and I am excited to see the big things you will accomplish.

Thirdly, the team at Palise Property – Jeff Palise, Liam Carmody and Tom Pettifer. Your continued hard work to ensure the best outcomes for our clients is inspiring, and it is a joy to work with you.

Finally, my fiancée Lisa. Your energy and enthusiasm for life means there is never a dull (or stationary) moment. I feel very lucky to receive your love and support.

To my friend Ian Marsden: you did not contribute or help with this book at all. But, as you are a slightly above average friend, and will like seeing your name printed, you get a mention.

INDEX

ALSO BY STEVE PALISE

Be better with business books

MAJOR STREET

We hope you enjoy reading this book. We'd love you to post a review on social media or your favourite bookseller site. Please include the hashtag #majorstreetpublishing.

Major Street Publishing specialises in business, leadership, personal finance and motivational non-fiction books. If you'd like to receive regular updates about new Major Street books, email info@majorstreet.com.au and ask to be added to our mailing list.

Visit majorstreet.com.au to find out more about our books (print, audio and ebooks) and authors, read reviews and find links to our Your Next Read podcast.

We'd love you to follow us on social media.

in linkedin.com/company/major-street-publishing

f facebook.com/MajorStreetPublishing

instagram.com/majorstreetpublishing

@MajorStreetPub